NEW OXFORD ENGLISH SERIES

General Editor: A. NORMAN JEFFARES

TENNYSON

SELECTED POEMS

Chosen and edited by

MICHAEL MILLGATE

OXFORD UNIVERSITY PRESS

Oxford University Press, Great Clarendon Street, Oxford OX2 6DP

Oxford New York
Athens Auckland Bangkok Bogota Bombay
Buenos Aires Calcutta Cape Town Dar es Salaam
Delhi Florence Hong Kong Istanbul Karachi
Kuala Lumpur Madras Madrid Melbourne
Mexico City Nairobi Paris Singapore
Taipei Tokyo Toronto Warsaw

and associated companies in
Berlin Ibadan

Oxford is a trade mark of Oxford University Press

Cover portrait by Leonard Rosoman

First published 1963
Reprinted 1996, 1973, 1975, 1978, 1979, 1983, 1987,
1989 (Twice), 1996, 1997

Printed in Hong Kong

CONTENTS

INTRODUCTION

I. TENNYSON: A BIOGRAPHICAL SKETCH

ALFRED TENNYSON was born on 6 August 1809, a few weeks before the fourteenth birthday of John Keats. Had Tennyson died young we would now think of him as one of the minor Romantics; in fact he lived on almost to span the century, dying at last, at the age of 83, in 1892, when W. B. Yeats was already twenty-seven and T. S. Eliot was a child of four. There are still people who remember Tennyson in his old age; we have many photographs of him, above all the magnificent studies by his friend Julia Cameron; we even have, astonishingly, a few recordings of his great voice thundering out the rhythms of such poems as 'The Charge of the Light Brigade' in a bardic chant remarkably similar to that of Yeats. It is true that over a century and a half have gone by since Tennyson was born, but we should not think of him as being farther away from us than he really is. We may no longer be able to take Tennyson very seriously as a philosopher-poet, but we should at least recognize the distinctively 'modern' character of many of the problems which faced him as a poet and of many of the questions which troubled him as a sensitive, thoughtful human being.

If Tennyson's birth seems remote in time, the place of his birth, the Rectory at Somersby, a hamlet in the heart of the Lincolnshire Wolds, will strike many people as having a comparable geographical remoteness. Tennyson's father, Dr. George Tennyson, was Rector of Somersby, and the Rectory itself still stands, although it is now a private house. It is a small, pleasant building, long and low, facing the church across a narrow lane. At the back the long garden, with its lawn, is almost surrounded by trees. Those who do not know Somersby often think of it in terms of the 'glooming flats' which Mariana saw from the window of the moated grange; in fact Tennyson had the good fortune to be born in one of the few areas of Lincolnshire which can justly be described as 'pretty' in accordance with the cosy English notion of what countryside should look like. Somersby is certainly isolated, and the 'glooming flats' of southern and eastern Lincolnshire are not far away, but the immediate neighbourhood is a charming place of copses and narrow lanes, protected by the wolds from the worst excesses of the easterly gales. Tennyson himself has left abundant evidence of his affection for Somersby: he calls it his 'sweet birth-place', the 'Home of my delight'; the attic where he wrote his early verse becomes his 'darling room'; and the Rectory garden is beautifully evoked as the setting for the crucial section xcv of *In Memoriam*.

Sir Harold Nicolson in his study of Tennyson poses a question that must have also occurred to other visitors to Somersby: just how was the family of eleven children, including seven boys almost all of whom grew to be at least six foot tall, ever crammed into that small house along with their parents and the family servants?[1] Sir Charles Tennyson, the poet's grandson, in his biography of Tennyson, mentions a letter of 1824 in which Dr. Tennyson complains that he has a family of twenty-three, sleeping five or six to a room.[2] Such intimacy brought great happiness at times, yet at others it must have encouraged inborn tendencies to morbidity and depression. These tendencies certainly existed. The Tennysons were an extremely handsome family—Alfred himself was, to the end, a magnificent figure of a man—but they were also a rather odd family.

[1] Harold Nicolson, *Tennyson: Aspects of his Life, Character and Poetry*, London, 1923, p. 33.
[2] Charles Tennyson, *Alfred Tennyson*, London, 1950, p. 46.

The poet's grandfather, George Clayton Tennyson, who lived some miles to the north in the enormous Gothic 'folly' of Bayons Manor, was a wealthy eccentric who, for reasons not fully apparent, decided to disinherit his elder son, George, in favour of his younger son, Charles. Instead of inheriting wealth, George Tennyson, the poet's father, found himself obliged to enter the church. He was an educated and in many ways an unusually gifted man, but he had little taste or affection for his pastoral duties, the grudge he bore his father became by gradual stages an obsession, and he succumbed eventually to alcoholism, accompanied by fits of violence. All of Dr. Tennyson's sons were eccentric in one way or another. Edward's progressive insanity made it necessary for him to be permanently confined; Charles took to opium for a time, Arthur to drink; while Sir Charles Tennyson recalls the story of Septimus rising from a recumbent position on the hearth-rug to greet an astonished visitor with the words: 'I am Septimus, the most morbid of the Tennysons.'[1] It seems clear, in fact, that the strong, dark strain of morbidity in Alfred's own work and personality formed part of a family pattern.

Obviously, Tennyson's childhood was far from being an entirely happy one. Its worst phase was probably the period from late 1815 to 1820 when he was enduring the brutal régime of Louth Grammar School, but the decline of Dr. Tennyson cast a deepening shadow over later years as well. Sir Charles Tennyson records that when Dr. Tennyson's drinking brought on paroxysms of violence Alfred would often 'run out and throw himself down among the graves in the churchyard, longing for death'.[2] Yet all the time Alfred was writing verse in astonishing quantity and, considering his age, of remarkable quality. Sir Charles Tennyson assigns to the years between 1820, when Alfred was eleven, and 1826, when

[1] Ibid., p. 199.   [2] Ibid., p. 48.

he was seventeen, such items as an epic of 6,000 lines in the style of Sir Walter Scott's *Marmion*, a blank verse fragment, about 500 lines long, entitled *Armageddon*, and at least two blank verse plays. After hearing of such activity we are not altogether surprised to find Tennyson, in collaboration with his elder brothers Charles and Frederick, venturing into print at the age of seventeen with a volume entitled *Poems by Two Brothers* (the volume was mainly the work of Alfred and Charles). The book was published by a local firm, Jacksons of Louth, whose moment of commercial rashness has been rewarded by a kind of immortality.

In 1828 Alfred and Charles went up to Trinity College, Cambridge, where Frederick was already in residence. At Cambridge Tennyson was strongly influenced by a group of earnest, high-minded young men who called themselves the Apostles; in 1829 he won the Chancellor's Medal for the prize poem *Timbuctoo*, an achievement which confirmed the Apostles in the belief that he was destined for fame and greatness as a poet; and in 1828 or early 1829 he met Arthur Hallam, a handsome and gifted young man whom his contemporaries, including Gladstone, continued to the end of their lives to regard as the outstanding genius of their generation. Tennyson and Hallam quickly formed a friendship which was both intimate and intense. In 1830, with Hallam's encouragement, Tennyson published *Poems, Chiefly Lyrical*, and in the summer of that year the two young men went to the Pyrenees on a wild mission to carry money and instructions to a group of revolutionaries who were hoping to overthrow the Spanish king. Early in 1831, to Tennyson's joy, Hallam became engaged to his sister Emily. Hallam's father, Henry Hallam, the historian, enforced a separation of twelve months, but when the year was up Hallam came to Somersby and all was happiness.

The happiness, however, was short-lived. In March 1831 Dr. Tennyson died and Alfred left Cambridge without taking his degree. In May 1832 John Wilson ('Christopher North') published in *Blackwood's Magazine*, of which he was editor, a review of *Poems, Chiefly Lyrical* which combined mingled praise and criticism of Tennyson's poems with vigorous abuse of an article in which Arthur Hallam had made rather exaggerated claims for his friend's work. Worse was to follow, for Tennyson's *Poems*, published by Edward Moxon in December 1832, was savagely attacked by John Wilson Croker, writing in the April issue of the *Quarterly Review*, the most influential periodical of the day. Tennyson, always excessively sensitive to adverse criticism, was deeply injured. But all the griefs and irritations were soon to be completely overshadowed by the sudden and totally unexpected death, on 15 September 1833, of Arthur Hallam, who was on a visit to Vienna with his father. Emily Tennyson, whom Hallam had intended to marry, suffered greatly; of Tennyson himself it is not too much to say that the death of Hallam was the single most important emotional experience of his life. At first he was distraught and longed for death, but by the end of the year he was again writing poetry and had already begun work on what eventually became *In Memoriam*, the tribute of his grief for his lost friend.

For nine years after 1833 Tennyson published almost nothing, and much of his time was taken up with rather desultory travelling in Britain and on the Continent. This was made possible by the modest bequests received by the Somersby family on the death in 1835 of George Clayton Tennyson, the bulk of the very considerable property going to the younger branch of the family. In 1837 Tennyson's mother and the children who remained at home moved from Somersby—where the Rectory was needed for a new incumbent—to High Beech, near Epping, Essex. Epping had the advantage of being near to London, and Tennyson now made frequent visits to the city. He renewed acquaintance with such Cambridge friends as Edward Fitzgerald, James Spedding, and Richard Monckton Milnes (later Lord Houghton), and made many new friends, including Thackeray, Gladstone, Landor, Macready (the actor), and Thomas Carlyle, who described Tennyson in 1840 as a 'fine, large-featured, dim-eyed, bronze-coloured, shaggy-headed man . . . dusty, smoky, free and easy . . . a most restful, brotherly, solid-hearted man'.[1] In 1840 the Tennysons moved to Tunbridge Wells, in Kent, and in the following year to Boxley, near Maidstone. Here they were within two miles of Park House, home of the Lushington family, and in *The Princess* he was to take as his setting a meeting of the local Mechanics' Institute in the grounds of Park House.

These were the years of Tennyson's courtship of Emily Sellwood, whom he had first met in 1830, and whom he met again in 1836 when she was bridesmaid at the marriage of her sister Louisa to Alfred's brother Charles. In 1838 Alfred and Emily were engaged, but two years later the engagement was broken off, largely because of the opposition of Emily's parents and Alfred's lack of a secure income. Tennyson's two-volume *Poems* of 1842 received a rather cool reception from the public and from most of the critics—though his reputation was growing steadily with a discriminating few both in England and in America—and in 1843 he lost all his capital, which he had invested in a scheme for wood-carving by machinery. This was an unhappy time for Tennyson. He became depressed and ill, and in 1844, after the family had moved to Cheltenham, he underwent the 'water cure' at a hydropathic hospital nearby. In 1845, however, he recovered much of the money he had lost in the wood-carving scheme

[1] Hallam, Lord Tennyson, *Alfred Lord Tennyson: A Memoir*, London, 1897, i. 187 n. In subsequent notes this work is referred to as *Memoir*.

and Sir Robert Peel, at the instigation of Henry Hallam, Arthur's father, granted him a Civil List pension of £200 a year. He made many new friends at this period, notably Charles Dickens, Coventry Patmore, and Francis Palgrave, and in 1847 he ventured into print again with *The Princess*. The poem was unpopular with the critics and with many of Tennyson's friends, but it had a much better sale than Tennyson's previous volumes. One important result of this improvement in his financial prospects was the renewal, late in 1849, of his correspondence with Emily Sellwood.

It was only in 1850, however, that Tennyson first tasted the success and fame that were to characterize the rest of his life. On 1 June of that year he published *In Memoriam*, which became an immediate 'best-seller'. The poem was published anonymously at first, but its authorship did not remain a secret for long; Tennyson quickly became a national figure, and in November he was made Poet Laureate in succession to Wordsworth, who had died in April. What finally marks 1850 as Tennyson's *annus mirabilis*, however, is its third great event, his marriage on 13 June to Emily Sellwood. The ceremony took place at Shiplake-on-Thames, where the vicar was Drummond Rawnsley, an old Lincolnshire friend, whose wife, a cousin of Emily's, had played a large part in bringing the couple together again. The renewal of the engagement had been facilitated both by Tennyson's improved economic position and by the appearance early in 1850 of the privately distributed *Fragments of an Elegy*, an early version of *In Memoriam*, which had persuaded Emily's parents of his reliability in religious matters. After the wedding they went first of all to visit Arthur Hallam's grave at Clevedon, Somerset; the suggestion was Emily's and it 'seemed a kind of consecration to go there'.[1]

[1] *Memoir*, i. 332.

Early in 1851 the Tennysons came to live at Chapel House,
Twickenham, where their son, Hallam, was born in August
1852. Emily's first child had been still-born the previous year,
but she was to have a second son, Lionel, in 1854. By that
time the family was living at Farringford, near Freshwater in
the Isle of Wight. Tennyson rented the house in 1853 and
bought it in 1856, attracted by the seclusion of the place, the
warmth of the climate, and the charms of the house and its
setting. Farringford itself is a low, grey, late Georgian building,
set among trees in the pleasant valley which runs inland from
Alum Bay near the western tip of the island. This is the place
most intimately associated with Tennyson's later career. It is
here that he played host to old friends such as Fitzgerald,
Clough, Edward Lear, and Jowett, to new friends living
nearby, notably Julia Cameron, Sir John Simeon, and William
Ward,[1] and to an ever-increasing number of the great and the
celebrated, from the Prince Consort to Garibaldi. It is here,
too, that Tennyson wrote most of the many poems of his
Laureate years, and some critics have seen in Farringford and
Somersby, with their differing climates, convenient symbols
of the contrast between Tennyson's earlier and later poetry;
they say that the early poetry is robust, as befitting Lincoln-
shire, the later poetry effete, as befitting the more southerly
Isle of Wight. It is easy to make too much of this: Farringford,
after all, is not Fez, nor even Florence. In so far as there was a
decline in Tennyson's later verse, the climate of Farringford
was a far less important factor than Tennyson's increasing
age, affluence, fame, and respectability, and above all the close,
coddling, intimate life that Emily so skilfully built up around
him. She herself kept in the background as much as possible,
but she ran everything: household, children, correspondence,

[1] For more details of Tennyson's friendships see Charles Tennyson, op. cit.,
especially pp. 266–7, 278–84, 323–6, 403–6.

business, entertainment—and, in the subtlest possible way, Alfred himself. Every load that could be lifted from Alfred's shoulders she gladly took on to her own, anxious that the poet should have the freedom to be nothing but a poet, the opportunity to exercise his gifts to the full. Alfred's principal annoyance, in fact, came to be the occasional inconveniences of fame —the pestering literary pilgrims, the inquisitive tourists who peered in over the garden fence or popped out from behind bushes when he took his walks on the downs. He seems to have had no desire for personal publicity and he certainly hated being regarded as one of the 'sights' of England that simply had to be seen by visiting Americans and colonials.

On the other hand he could hardly exist without admiration. He needed desperately the approval of his family, his friends, and his fellow writers. He was deeply hurt by adverse criticism, and one of Emily's self-imposed tasks was to prevent his catching sight of unfavourable reviews. In his later years he was perpetually surrounded, one might almost say engulfed, by admiration, approval, flattery, and scarcely allowed to catch a discordant note in the great chorus of adulation. Although widely regarded as a kind of national hero and national oracle, a man of great wisdom and experience and of almost prophetic vision, Tennyson led in fact an extremely narrow, sheltered, and 'managed' life, and was rarely brought into contact with those trivia of human intercourse and daily living that we think of as constituting 'reality'. It is a remarkable picture, and a sad one: Emily's devotion set Alfred free, but in a kind of vacuum. Emily is not in the least a sinister figure, and no more than the Farringford climate can she alone be blamed for the comparative failure of much of the later poetry: there seems little doubt, however, that in seeking to defend her husband's sensitivities she innocently contributed to the decline of his genius.

In the last thirty years or so of Tennyson's life volumes of poems and plays continued to appear with astonishing frequency, but other events of major significance were comparatively few. In 1868, annoyed by the constant intrusions on his privacy at Farringford, he began building a house at Aldworth, near Haslemere; when the house was completed he generally spent the summer months there, wintering at Farringford as usual. In 1874 Emily fell ill and Hallam came home from Cambridge to act as his father's secretary and *amanuensis*. Later years were disturbed by the deaths of old friends—Julia Cameron and his brother Charles in 1879, for instance, Drummond Rawnsley and James Spedding in 1881, W. G. Ward in 1882—but the worst blow was the death of his son Lionel, on his way home from India, in 1886. In 1888 Tennyson himself had a serious attack of rheumatic gout and his life was feared for. He made a remarkable recovery, however—his famous poem 'Crossing the Bar' was written during his convalescence and it was in 1890 that the recordings of his voice were made—and death did not come until 1892, when, on 6 October, the old poet passed away at the age of eighty-three, still in full possession of his faculties, his Shakespeare in his hand. Six days later came the triumphal funeral at Westminster Abbey, the nation's tribute to a dead hero.

II. TENNYSON'S IDEAS AND BELIEFS

Tennyson at the height of his fame enjoyed a popularity such as no other English poet has enjoyed in his lifetime, such perhaps as no other poet has ever enjoyed. He was not merely the Poet Laureate, he was *the* poet; as G. M. Young puts it, 'Tennyson was The Poet: and to the people poetry was what Tennyson wrote.'[1] Such a reputation did not, could not, last.

[1] G. M. Young, 'The Age of Tennyson', in *Today and Yesterday*, London, 1948, p. 44.

Tennyson himself seems to have foreseen this: 'Modern fame is nothing,' he is reported to have said, 'I'd rather have an acre of land. I shall go down, down! I'm up now. Action and reaction.'[1] And so it has been. The reaction began even before Tennyson's death, as the popularity of Swinburne and other younger poets clearly suggests. After 1892 the reaction became strong and obvious, though it was primarily a reaction against the philosophy and attitudes of Tennyson's work, its representative Victorian quality, rather than the poetic craftsmanship: Tennyson, as a 'nature poet', was still a living influence for the Georgians even at the moment when his reputation was being involved in that general debunking of the Victorians which culminated in Lytton Strachey's *Eminent Victorians* (1918).

It is clear, at least, that the violence of the reaction against Tennyson derived largely from the fact that Victorian admiration for him had been rooted not so much in appreciation of his distinctive qualities as a poet as in gratitude for the comfort and encouragement he offered as a thinker and teacher. Matthew Arnold wrote in 1860 that Tennyson 'with all his temperament and artistic skill, is deficient in intellectual power; and no modern poet can make very much of his business unless he is pre-eminently strong in this'.[2] Arnold was not alone in this view, even among his contemporaries, but the great weight of Victorian opinion, from T. H. Huxley downwards, concurred in regarding Tennyson as a philosopher and seer, the supreme interpreter of his age, 'the Great Voice of Victorian England'.[3] And this, of course, is the one aspect of Tennyson which the twentieth century has been unable to take seriously.

[1] *Memoir*, i. 513.

[2] Quoted in F. L. Lucas (ed.), *Tennyson: Poetry and Prose*, Oxford, 1947, p. xxxiii.

[3] Quoted in Hallam. Lord Tennyson (ed.), *Tennyson and His Friends*, London, 1911, p. 185.

Tennyson was very much aware of the intellectual currents of his time. He read widely in the contemporary literature of science, geology, and astronomy, and he gave much thought to the condition of Victorian society and to the directions in which that society was likely to develop. Too much has been made of his not especially original prophecies of aerial warfare and world government in *Locksley Hall*; yet these do suggest a characteristic of the poem as a whole, that it could only have been written by an alert and well-informed mind which was acutely receptive to contemporary ideas and attitudes. The final effect of the poem is confused and ambiguous, largely because the speaker of this dramatic monologue is a sensitive but arrogant and somewhat unbalanced young man who is clearly not to be directly identified with Tennyson himself. The ambiguity, however, is itself an indication of the way in which Tennyson's lack of intellectual strength may actually give his work a special interest for the modern reader, not only because it often reflects so directly, even naively, the changing mood of the period (see, for example, such 'Laureate' poems as the 'Ode sung at the Opening of the International Exhibition' and the verses 'To the Queen' which appear at the end of the *Idylls of the King*), but also because its constant ambiguity and self-contradiction may serve to direct our attention to the deep divisions and instabilities within the whole Victorian edifice.

In Tennyson's religious and philosophical poems the voice of doubt is always heard, because it was so loud and so insistent that it could not be silenced, yet the poems themselves end almost always on a note of optimism. It was unthinkable, inconceivable, that they should do otherwise. God had to exist because without him nothing made sense. There is an unresolved conflict in all of Tennyson's religious verse from the beginning to the end of his career, and in 'The Two Voices' this conflict is explicitly dramatized in the form of a dialogue between the 'I' of the poem, whom it seems safe to identify with the poet, and the bitter voice of disillusionment and despair. While the discussion is confined to earthly existence the voice of despair clearly has the upper hand, and every argument against suicide is crushingly refuted. But when the discussion moves to the question of immortality the voice is silenced, not so much by the argument (in lines 289–309) that man finds in his soul ideas of eternity and perfection which cannot be realized on earth and which must therefore have an existence elsewhere, as by the vague evidence of 'mystic gleams' and by the appearance of a staid Victorian family making its way to church. Towards the end of the poem a new voice speaks encouragingly of 'A hidden hope', generating the feeling, which unhappily cannot be verified ('altho' no tongue can prove'), that

> every cloud, that spreads above
> And veileth love, itself is love.

Similarly, at the end of 'The Vision of Sin' we are told that 'God made Himself an awful rose of dawn'; at the end of 'Vastness', a very late poem, the catalogue of negations is closed with the abrupt reversal:

> Peace, let it be! for I loved him, and love him
> for ever: the dead are not dead but alive.

In such poems the conflict between the need to believe and the difficulty of believing is all too plain, and Tennyson is seen to be clinging almost desperately to the central, indispensable belief that our life on earth is meaningless without the hope of immortality. This is the essence, and almost the sum, of his position. He was not concerned to uphold the dogmas of historical Christianity: the concluding stanza of *In Memoriam*, for example, is certainly affirmative but it does not seem to be specifically Christian:

> That God, which ever lives and loves,
>   One God, one law, one element,
>   And one far-off divine event,
> To which the whole creation moves.

This doctrinal indefiniteness seems not to have troubled Tennyson's readers. It was enough for them that the poet, while sharing all the doubts and fears of an age shaken by new scientific discoveries, by theories of evolution, by historical criticism of the Bible, and by a general collapse of the old religious, ethical, and social certainties, had nevertheless emerged with some kind of religious conviction still intact. One of the reasons for the enormous popularity of *In Memoriam* must surely have been the way in which the poet's religious doubts, before being overcome, were given a full and even eloquent hearing. The poem became a kind of national confessional, with a comfortable absolution at the end.

Tennyson's great strength, at least in the eyes of his contemporaries, was the fact that he did not ignore or reject the new theory of evolution nor any of the evidence of modern science. C. F. G. Masterman makes this point in his *Tennyson as Religious Teacher*, which remains the best and fullest treatment of this particular aspect of Tennyson's work:

He accepted all facts as facts, acknowledging that it is impossible to fight against the convictions of the human reason. All the conclusions of modern science and modern criticism, however unpalatable their results, however desperate their apparent tendencies, he recognised and welcomed. So that, in a sense, men were compelled to acknowledge that Tennyson at least faced the problems of the age; that he did not refuse to acknowledge facts because they disagreed with his own theories; that he did not twist facts to suit his own prejudices; that in the region of thought he was emphatically *'no skulker'*.[1]

It is vain to search for Tennyson's 'philosophy', for he did not have one: he never arrived at any coherent system of reasoned attitudes and beliefs. At the same time, almost all his poetry is conditioned by his need to believe, his desperate search for confirmation of a faith which was always precarious though never lost. The effect is sometimes valuable, as in the visionary moment so movingly described in section xcv of *In Memoriam*, but often the sense of being on the edge of chaos leads only to an exaggeration of familiar Victorian attitudes: one thinks, for example, of the too-strident patriotism and exaltation of war found in *Maud*; of his frequent celebrations of Victorian family life and of male superiority; and of his rather chilling insistence on the qualities of 'Self-reverence, self-knowledge, self-control' in the presentation of such heroes as King Arthur.

There is no doubt that Tennyson came increasingly to look upon himself as the prophet and interpreter of his age, and he was certainly encouraged in this conception of himself by the adulation of his friends and by the popularity of his religious and didactic works. Modern readers, of course, have generally agreed in finding this the most regrettable aspect of Tennyson's later career, but it is worth bearing in mind the cautionary words of Sir Harold Nicolson:

The age of Tennyson was an age of real spiritual agony ... a poet would have indeed been limited and selfish if he had failed to the extent of his capacity to respond to the crying spiritual needs of his contemporaries. We may regret that Tennyson clung so timidly to the sedate and middle course, we may feel angered at his material prosperity being built up on foundations which appear to us unsound

[1] C. F. G. Masterman, *Tennyson as a Religious Teacher*, London, 1899, p. 240.

and insincere, but we must remember that the poetry of Tennyson, even those many pieces which we now deride, brought great solace to many unhappy people, and we must admit that even if, to us, his thought seems shallow and insincere, it was hailed by millions of his countrymen as penetrating, audacious and profound.[1]

III. TENNYSON: A CRITICAL APPRECIATION

Sir Harold Nicolson finds words to explain and to some extent justify Tennyson's peculiar relationship to his age, but it is clear that, as a twentieth-century critic, he has little real sympathy with the poet in his role as interpreter and sage. More recent critics have been even less sympathetic, and a particularly harsh judgement is expressed by Paull F. Baum in his *Tennyson Sixty Years After*:

There can be no doubt that Tennyson applied himself earnestly to the duty, once it had been revealed to him, of playing demiurge to the *Zeitgeist*. . . . For Tennyson, wanting both through the emotional poverty of his private life and through the absence of inner fire and spiritual energy, here was the very thing, a thrice welcome opportunity. Art, meaning skill and craftsmanship, he already had and he was learning swiftly to improve his native gift; what he needed was matter. His task then was to understand and reveal to his readers the true inwardness of his age. For more than forty years he was its Laureate. It was an impossible task, certainly, for a sensitive and reclusive man, with a strong inherited melancholy, disinclined to face the slings and arrows of the critics, and with only mediocre intellectual endowment.[2]

An opposing view is to be found in the final paragraph of Jerome Hamilton Buckley's *Tennyson: The Growth of a Poet*:

Laureate for nearly half a century to one of the world's great ages, Tennyson commanded such public attention as no English writer

[1] Nicolson, op. cit., p. 11.

[2] Paull F. Baum, *Tennyson Sixty Years After*, Chapel Hill, North Carolina, [1948], pp. vi–vii.

before or since has known. Sensitive to the moral and spiritual con-
fusions of his time, familiar with the new sciences, aware of imminent
social change and crisis, he was the voice and sometimes indeed the
conscience of Victorian culture; and his work will endure, even apart
from its aesthetic worth, as a mirror of his civilization. Yet the dis-
tinction that his critics have repeatedly drawn between the bard of
public sentiments and the earlier poet of private sensibilities is ulti-
mately untenable. For there was no real break in Tennyson's career;
from the beginning he felt some responsibility to the society he lived
in, and until the end he remained obedient to the one clear call of his
own imagination. His development depended not on a sacrifice of
the personal vision, but on the constant interaction between public
knowledge and private feeling. From first to last his best poetry
raised a psychological protest against the commonplace fact he knew
with the intellect or acutely perceived with the senses. In the per-
spectives of evolutionary theory, he saw perpetual movement as the
law of life; but with all his own passion of the past, he intuited a
lost order of values, a peace—both aesthetic and religious—untouched
by the bewildering changefulness and relativity of the world. Behind
the roar of the London street, he could imagine what once had been
'the stillness of the central sea,' the elemental reality with which the
spirit must once again come to terms. His response to the restless
activity of his time enhanced rather than weakened his concern with
the moment of insight and revelation. And his art at its highest,
transcending change, invested the transitory with meaning and
purpose.[1]

In referring to those critics who have distinguished between
'the bard of public sentiments and the earlier poet of private
sensibilities' Buckley presumably has particularly in mind Sir
Harold Nicolson and F. L. Lucas, both of whom praise the
early Tennyson at the expense of the later and take Somersby
and Farringford as symbols of the two phases in the poet's

[1] Jerome Hamilton Buckley, *Tennyson: The Growth of a Poet*, Cambridge,
Mass., and London, 1960, pp. 255–6.

career. Nicolson concludes his study by firmly rejecting Tennyson the Laureate in favour of Tennyson the 'morbid and unhappy mystic',[1] the sensitive, subjective poet of loneliness and despair. Somersby is preferred to Farringford:

The age of Tennyson is past; the ideals which he voices so earnestly have fallen from esteem. The day may come, perhaps, when the conventions of that century will once again inspire the thoughtful or animate the weak. But, for the moment, it is not through these that any interest can be evoked. And thus, if we consider it reasonable and right that Tennyson should also stand among the poets, let us, for the present, forget the delicate Laureate of a cautious age; the shallow thought, the vacant compromise; the honeyed idyll, the complacent ode; let us forget the dulled monochrome of his middle years, forget the magnolia and the roses, the indolent Augusts of his island-home; forget the laurels and the rhododendrons.

Let us recall only the low booming of the North Sea upon the dunes; the grey clouds lowering above the wold; the moan of the night wind on the fen; the far glimmer of marsh-pools through the reeds; the cold, the half-light, and the gloom.[2]

In these quotations we may perceive the outlines of the main approaches towards Tennyson which have been adopted by modern critics. Nicolson sees it as his task to rescue Tennyson from himself and from his age, to identify and celebrate those limited aspects of his work which can still be appreciated by modern readers. Baum's conclusions are substantially in line with Nicolson's, but he differs considerably over points of detail, and his argument, supported by far more analysis of particular poems, is generally more hostile to Tennyson. Buckley, on the other hand, completely rejects Nicolson's position and starts from the assumption that Tennyson is a great poet. These critics have all made valuable contributions to our knowledge and understanding of Tennyson's work;

[1] Nicolson, op. cit., p. 27.   [2] Ibid., p. 303.

the differences between them, however, show just how widely critical estimates of Tennyson continue to diverge. There is still no general consensus of opinion as to whether or not Tennyson is a great poet, or even a good one, and it is perhaps best to try to approach Tennyson's poetry with as few pre-conceptions as possible, and to allow one's personal judgement to operate freely on the basis of a close and careful reading of the poems themselves.

About the very early poetry there is likely to be comparatively little disagreement: few, at least, will dissent from the view that it is a very remarkable and very precocious achievement. Tennyson was probably only fourteen when he wrote these lines from his verse-play *The Devil and the Lady*; the Devil speaks:

> Yon taper sinks i' th' socket; Time wears quickly,
> Yet treads in shoes of felt. What is't o'clock?
> > [*Going to the timepiece*
> Half after midnight! These mute moralizers,
> Pointing to the unheeded lapse of hours,
> Become a tacit eloquent reproach
> Unto the dissipation of this Earth.
> There is a clock in Pandemonium,
> Hard by the burning throne of my Great Grandsire,
> The slow vibrations of whose pendulum,
> With click-clack alternation to and fro,
> Sound 'EVER, NEVER!' thro' the courts of Hell,
> Piercing the wrung ears of the damn'd that writhe
> Upon their beds of flame, and, whensoe'er
> There may be short cessation of their wailings,
> Through all the boundless depth of fires is heard
> The shrill and solemn warning 'EVER, NEVER.'
> Then bitterly, I trow, they turn and toss
> And shriek and shout, to drown the thrilling note—
> > [*Looking again at the timepiece*

> Half after midnight! Wherefore stand I here?
> Methinks my tongue runs twenty knots an hour:
> I must unto mine office.   [*Exit abruptly*

Remarkable and precocious as these lines are, they are curiously unlike most of Tennyson's subsequent work, although we do catch a somewhat similar note in the plays Tennyson wrote late in life, and especially in his best play, *Becket*. Obviously the passage is indebted, especially for its vocabulary, to Milton, Shakespeare, and the Elizabethan dramatists generally, and it can simply be argued that Tennyson was subject in later years to quite different literary influences. But the verse is not mere pastiche: one notes, for example, the 'wit'—paradoxical if not especially subtle—of 'tacit eloquent reproach'; the use of 'dissipation' with a full awareness of its two meanings of 'intemperance' and 'dissolution'; and, in lines 7–13, the precision of verse-movement which 'fits the sense' without indulging in the too insistent 'effects' of much of the later verse.

What Tennyson exhibits in his early verse is simply an instinctive feeling for rhythm and movement, a marvellous responsiveness and openness to language and its metaphorical possibilities, an exuberant talent which is the more obvious for its spontaneity and lack of sophistication. The exuberance shows itself most clearly, perhaps, in passages of humour and sheer fun, as when the magician Magus comes upon the Devil dressed in women's clothes:

> How now, my Hellish Minister, dark child
> Of bottomless Hades; what rude waggery
> What jejune undigested joke is this?
> To quilt thy fuscous haunches with the flounc'd,
> Frilled, finical delicacy of female dress.
> How hast thou dar'd to girdle thy brown sides
> And prop thy monstrous vertebrae with stays?
> Speak out, thou petticoated Solecism.

Some of the most attractive qualities of this early verse seem to be largely absent from the mature poems with which we are familiar: the almost boisterous humour, for example, the verbal adventurousness involving exploitation of ambiguity and paradox, and the readiness to employ imagery that is specific and concrete, as in the passage just quoted, rather than 'atmospheric'. It is hard to resist the suspicion that these qualities did not simply drop out of Tennyson's later work but were deliberately removed, conscientiously disciplined away.

Texts of the early poems in the present selection derive from the form in which they appeared in the 1842 edition of Tennyson's work, although some of them had appeared in a different form in *Poems, Chiefly Lyrical* of 1830 or in the *Poems* of 1832. We still know comparatively little of Tennyson's poetic activities during the 'years of silence' between 1833 and 1842; they must have been considerable, however, and seem to have involved nothing less than a deliberate attempt on Tennyson's part to remake himself as a poet, with the aim of achieving critical approval, if not general popularity. The attempt seems to have been largely stimulated by the criticisms of his early work which had appeared in *Blackwood's*, the *Quarterly*, and elsewhere,[1] and one of its most important and most obvious results was the elimination of 'wildness' and 'obscurity'—seen, for example, in a poem like 'The Hesperides', printed in 1832 but suppressed in 1842—despite the fact that these qualities had been, at least in part, a sign of verbal and intellectual adventurousness. It also involved the bringing to artistic perfection of those poems which were considered safe for republication, a process only accomplished at the cost of some vigour and spontaneity. The 1842 edition is clearly a much greater and more consistent achievement than

[1] See Edgar Finley Shannon, Jr., *Tennyson and the Reviewers*, Cambridge, Mass., 1952.

the edition of 1832, but it is at least arguable that by 1842 something valuable and vital had disappeared from Tennyson's work. But this is not to argue, however, that the 'Somersby' Tennyson is the 'real' Tennyson and that what comes afterwards is worthless by comparison. If something had been lost, much had been gained. Tennyson underwent a very considerable artistic development between 1832 and 1842, even though it was development along lines rather different from those promised by the early verse.

The edition of 1842, at all events, was to be the richest and most impressive of all Tennyson's publications, *In Memoriam* not excepted. The first of the two volumes consisted almost entirely of revised versions of poems previously published, including 'The Lady of Shalott', 'Oenone', 'Mariana', 'The Lotos-Eaters', and 'The Palace of Art'. The first four of these poems are all closely related to literary originals, they are very clearly 'Romantic' poems with the creation of a particular mood as one of their primary objectives, and they treat, in one way or another, the theme of withdrawal from the world. They provide some support, in fact, for the view that Tennyson at this time was a self-conscious artist who sought isolation from society through the creation of a dream-world. 'The Palace of Art' is explicitly dedicated to the proposition that the life of aesthetic withdrawal is wrong and must be rejected; as F. R. Leavis has observed, however, the celebration of the soul's enjoyment of a rich world of imagination is much more effective, as poetry, than the pointing of the explicit moral.[1] Indeed, the poem, not included in this selection, is extremely uneven in quality, though interesting as an illustration of the struggle between Tennyson's desire for a withdrawal from the world and his sense that this was not the proper role for a poet of the nineteenth century.

[1] F. R. Leavis, *New Bearings in English Poetry*, London, 1942, p. 16.

The official 'message' of 'The Palace of Art' seemed more arbitrary in the context of the 1832 edition than it did when the poem reappeared in the edition of 1842, since the second volume of that edition, devoted almost exclusively to poems which had not previously been published, contained several poems which plainly showed some kind of social awareness. For example, 'Morte d'Arthur'—later to be absorbed with very minor changes into 'The Passing of Arthur', the closing section of *The Idylls of the King*—adapts a crucial episode in the Arthurian story to the purposes of moral, religious, and even political statement:

> 'The old order changeth, yielding place to new,
> And God fulfils Himself in many ways,
> Lest one good custom should corrupt the world.'

Progress, it appears, is God-ordained, beneficial, and necessary. It is true that Arthur admits to a doubt about what will happen to him after death, but the tone of Arthur's speech as a whole remains assured, serene—and a little sactimonious: the compulsion for the poet to address the world about the world's problems emerges, and not for the last time in Tennyson's verse, as the voice of the preacher. Yet there are doubts and hesitations dramatized within the poem itself, mainly through the presentation of the puzzled, conscience-tormented, and ultimately lonely figure of Sir Bedivere, and these have much in common with the doubts and hesitations dramatized, explicitly or implicitly, in 'The Two Voices', 'Locksley Hall', and 'The Vision of Sin', all of which first appeared in 1842.

Most critics have seen no traces of doubt in 'Ulysses', the greatest of the poems first printed in 1842, yet it is hard to accept the poem as quite the unqualified assertion of purposeful optimism that it is generally taken to be. Tennyson, it is true, said that 'Ulysses' was 'written soon after Arthur Hallam's death, and it gives the feeling about the need of going forward and braving the struggle of life perhaps more simply than anything in *In Memoriam*'[1] and there is no doubt an allusion to Hallam, and one which is all the more moving for its simplicity and reticence, in the reference to 'the great Achilles, whom we knew'. But 'Ulysses' is a dramatic monologue, not a statement by Tennyson in his own person, and that fact must never be lost sight of. No one would think of identifying Tennyson with St. Simeon Stylites, the proud ascetic on his pillar, or Browning with Bishop Blougram, yet it is equally dangerous to assume too readily that Tennyson is speaking directly through such a first-person character as Ulysses.

The poem is magnificent in the simplicity and dignity of the language and the absolute assurance of the verse movement, and Ulysses emerges as a splendid and heroic figure. We are stirred, and rightly, by the final declaration of determination and courage. A careful reading of the poem makes it plain, however, that these qualities, though fine in themselves, are celebrated by Ulysses at the expense of other qualities which may ultimately be of even greater value, and which are certainly more desirable in any social context. It also seems clear that, in view of the age of Ulysses, his heroism, for all its magnificence, has a certain admixture of pathos, and some support for this view can be found in the key-lines of 'Tithonus', often regarded as a companion poem to 'Ulysses' and written at about the same time in the early eighteen-thirties, although it was not printed until 1860. The lines run:

> Why should a man desire in any way
> To vary from the kindly race of men,
> Or pass beyond the goal of ordinance
> Where all should pause, as is most meet for all?

[1] Tennyson, Annotation to Eversley Edition of his works, London, 1907–8; *Poems*, ii. 339.

'Tithonus', of course, is also a dramatic monologue, yet the poem may conceivably have some relevance as a cautionary tale pointing up the criticism and judgement of Ulysses which is implicit in the kind of individualistic programme he advances and the kind of realities and responsibilities he rejects.

Another dramatic monologue of this period, and one much closer in every way to Browning's ironic achievements in this particular form, is 'St. Simeon Stylites', the self-revelation of a pillar-squatting ascetic whose long years of well-publicized self-denial have brought him to a state, not of humility and grace, but of consuming spiritual pride. The note of sardonic humour in this poem appears again in 'The Vision of Sin', another of the poems which, like 'St. Simeon Stylites', first appeared in 1842. In the fourth section of 'The Vision of Sin' the narrator's dream of a young poet who has abandoned himself to voluptuousness is suddenly replaced by a second dream in which the poet, now grown old, arrives at a desolate inn and sings a bitter, cynical, and often macabre song of the vanity of human wishes and human ideals:

> 'Death is king, and Vivat Rex!
>   Tread a measure on the stones,
> Madam—if I know your sex,
>   From the fashion of your bones.'

But Tennyson also has a gentler, warmer humour. This is evident in the 1842 edition in 'Will Waterproof's Lyrical Monologue', and it re-emerges in 1847 in *The Princess*, a long narrative poem about a university for women and the eventual conquest of love over the claims of the female intellect. Despite the comic qualities of *The Princess*, the ideas in the poem which relate to 'the woman question' are taken quite seriously by Tennyson. It is true that these ideas do not ultimately appear in a particularly favourable light, but the poem is by no means an easy sneer at the movement for women's rights. John Kill-ham, indeed, in his most informative study, *Tennyson and The Princess*, makes out an excellent case for his view that '*The Princess*, properly understood, is a vivid reflection of an age. This is far from saying that it is a sort of literary photograph. What we have is, I think, more rare: a glimpse of the aspirations of the age in the colours in which they presented themselves to a truly poetic imagination.'[1]

The Princess remained for many years one of the most popular of Tennyson's works, and it can still be read through with pleasure, but most modern readers and critics have agreed in finding the valuable parts of the poem to be the interspersed lyrics, several of which were not added until the third edition of 1850. The best of these—'Tears, idle tears', 'The splendour falls on castle walls', 'Come down, O maid, from yonder mountain height', and 'Now sleeps the crimson petal, now the white'—represent one aspect of Tennyson's genius at its fullest development. Admittedly 'Come down, O maid', which opens finely with the authentic singing quality of the true lyric, has declined by the close into mere technical jugglery:

> The moan of doves in immemorial elms,
> And murmuring of innumerable bees.

But 'Now sleeps the crimson petal', despite its artificiality, achieves a delicate perfection scarcely equalled in English poetry—except by Marvell, whom Tennyson greatly admired —and it contains at least one miraculous line:

> Now lies the Earth all Danaë to the stars.

Tennyson does not often have this fusion of lyrical and intellectual qualities. It is a combination almost entirely absent

[1] John Killham, *Tennyson and The Princess*, London, 1958, pp. 3–4.

from *Maud*, for example, although the lyric gift alone is very much in evidence—notably in these lines from which the whole poem sprang:

> O that 'twere possible
> After long grief and pain
> To find the arms of my true love
> Round me once again!

We sense in *Maud*, however, the artificiality which mars the lyrics from *The Princess*. Even the lines just quoted lack the fierce spontaneity of the old poem which surely inspired them:

> Western wind, when wilt thou blow
> The small rain down can rain?
> Christ, that my love were in my arms
> And I in my bed again.

Tennyson's indebtedness here seems to be confirmed by the rhyme on 'again' and by the appearance, a few lines farther on in *Maud*, of the line:

> Ah Christ, that it were possible.

Although *Maud* contains a number of individual poems and passages of beauty and power, it is, as a whole, a somewhat artificial and even arbitrary construction. Tennyson called it a 'Monodrama', and it is a collection of short poems connected by the narrative thread of the hero's love for the beautiful Maud, his social superior though his childhood playmate, who lives 'up at the Hall', the great house of the village. Their love has a disastrous outcome when Maud's brother, 'That oil'd and curl'd Assyrian Bull', surprises the lovers at their tryst in the darkness of the Hall garden and is shot by the hero in a duel. The hero is forced to flee to France, and his mental instability, which has been evident from the first, degenerates

into madness. Later, however, he restores his mental health
and purges his guilt by going off to fight in the Crimean War.
The hero of this somewhat lurid episode voices powerful pro-
tests against social injustice and inequality:

> Sick, am I sick of a jealous dread?
> Was not one of the two at her side
> This new-made lord, whose splendour plucks
> The slavish hat from the villager's head?
> Whose old grandfather has lately died,
> Gone to a blacker pit, for whom
> Grimy nakedness dragging his trucks
> And laying his trams in a poison'd gloom
> Wrought, till he crept from a glutted mine
> Master of half a servile shire,
> And left his coal all turn'd into gold
> To a grandson, first of his noble line,
> Rich in the grace all women desire,
> Strong in the power that all men adore,
> And simper and set their voices lower,
> And soften as if to a girl, and hold
> Awe-stricken breaths at a work divine,
> Seeing his gewgaw castle shine,
> New as his title, built last year,
> There amid perky larches and pine,
> And over the sullen-purple moor
> (Look at it) pricking a cockney ear.

'If Tennyson has a single *worst* line,' writes Paull F. Baum,[1]
it is 'Whose old grandfather has lately died'. But the satirical
effectiveness of the passage as a whole cannot be doubted. It
strikes a note heard all too rarely in Tennyson's work, and in
imagery and intellectual content it has more in common with
the early verse of *The Devil and the Lady* than with most of his

---

[1] Baum, op. cit., p. 139.

mature poems. The actual impact of the satire, of course, is greatly reduced by the presentation of the hero as partly or wholly insane, but it is not surprising that popular reaction to the poem should have been extremely cool. Swinburne thought it 'the poem of the deepest charm and fullest delight, pathos and melody ever written'[1] but few seem to have agreed with him. Sir Charles Tennyson writes:

Alfred had thrown the whole passion of his being into *Maud*, which remained through life his favourite poem, the one which he loved best to read aloud and read with the most overwhelming effect. He had never written with more fire or originality, or given his genius freer rein, and he had high hopes of its reception. Unfortunately, these were doomed to bitter disappointment. The public were frankly bewildered, and indeed nothing could be imagined more different from the poem, which had won him his high position with the English people, *In Memoriam*.[2]

The Princess and *Maud* are now remembered chiefly for their lyrics, and when we turn to *In Memoriam*, published three years after *The Princess* and five years before *Maud*, we find Tennyson relying almost entirely upon his lyric and elegiac gifts for the success of what was to be, in many ways, the most important and most ambitious work of his life. The poem, which was devoted to the expression of his grief for Arthur Hallam, grew from the series of unrelated elegies on which he worked, off and on, for almost seventeen years following Hallam's death. When *In Memoriam* was finally published, however, the constituent poems were arranged in such a way as to demonstrate what Tennyson called 'The Way of the Soul', a two and a half year progress from the initial reaction of shock and horror of bereavement to the final celebration of love triumphant. A. C. Bradley attempted to explicate this

[1] *Memoir*, i. 425 n.
[2] Charles Tennyson, *Alfred Tennyson*, p. 285.

scheme in his *Commentary on In Memoriam*; his book is helpful,
but the exact progress of the 'The Way of the Soul' remains
unclear.

In an admiring essay on *In Memoriam* T. S. Eliot insists that
the poem cannot be properly approached through a few ex-
cerpted passages but must be read in its entirety: '*In Memoriam*
is the whole poem. It is unique: it is a long poem made by
putting together lyrics, which have only the unity and con-
tinuity of a diary, the concentrated diary of a man confessing
himself. It is a diary of which we have to read every word.'[1]
Eliot's view of the poem as a diary perhaps allows too little
weight to the impersonal, generalized, and philosophical
aspects of *In Memoriam* to which Tennyson himself drew
attention.

It must be remembered [he wrote], that this is a poem, *not* an actual
biography. It is founded on our friendship, on the engagement of
Arthur Hallam to my sister, on his sudden death at Vienna, just be-
fore the time fixed for their marriage, and on his burial at Clevedon
Church. The poem concludes with the marriage of my youngest sister
Cecilia [her husband was Edmund Lushington]. It was meant to be a
kind of *Divina Commedia*, ending with happiness. The sections were
written at many different places, and as the phases of our intercourse
came to my memory and suggested them. I did not write them with
any view of weaving them into a whole, or for publication, until I
found that I had written so many. The different moods of sorrow as in
a drama are dramatically given, and my conviction that fear, doubts,
and suffering will find answer and relief only through Faith in a God of
Love. 'I' is not always the author speaking of himself, but the voice of
the human race speaking thro' him.[2]

Paull F. Baum, after quoting part of this passage, reminds us
that Cecilia is not the sister who was to have married Arthur

---

[1] T. S. Eliot, *Selected Essays*, London, 1951, pp. 333–4.
[2] *Memoir*, i. 304–5.

Hallam, and notes that 'the poem is, on the poet's own testimony, partly personal and partly impersonal—"the voice of the human race"; but it is left for our own tact to distinguish the two voices'.[1] Baum believes that the 'form of the poem *as elegy* is well fitted both to the subject and to Tennyson's genius. For a record of sorrowing moments and personal memories the method—short lyrics without noticeable connection—is well chosen.'[2] But he feels that the personal and 'universal' elements are too much confused, that many of the autobiographical elements are not transmuted into poetry or integrated with the speculative aspect of the poem. As a philosophical poem, in short, *In Memoriam* 'lacks form and coherence . . . and it lacks that clearness and sureness of treatment which its subject emphatically demands':

The form, a series of short lyrics, is not suited to a sustained philosophical poem. The plan, a discontinuous record of incidents, moods, and meditations, is fatally improper to a serious presentation of one of the most difficult and profound subjects which interest the human mind and spirit; and Tennyson's own confession (or boast) of the casual way in which the poem grew would be sufficient, if internal evidence were not abundant, to condemn his method. For such a subject only a carefully plotted and clearly articulated plan could hope to succeed; yet Tennyson's plan was, having let his little memorial poems accumulate until they were numerous enough to publish, to give them the appearance of order by indicating a few dates and grouping them as best he could on a theoretical thread of grief, doúbt, hope, and faith. The series of lyrics shows a kind of progress, to be sure, but it is so frequently interrupted and diverted that the reader is constantly left in uncertainty. Tennyson might better have claimed less than he did in this respect; but he was tempted beyond his strength when he saw his poem's popular success.[3]

*   *   *   *

[1] Baum, op. cit., p. 120.   [2] Ibid.
[3] Ibid., p. 124.

Some of the emotions, some of the experiences, some of the findings of 'In Memoriam' *are* of universal application, and by them parts of the poem will live; but as a single poem it has had its day and ceased to be.[1]

Most modern readers are likely to feel some sympathy with Baum's criticisms of the philosophical aspects of the poem, but many will agree rather with Eliot at least to the extent of thinking that the poem gains greatly in impressiveness when it is read as a whole, even if all parts of it are not equally distinguished. Few, at any rate, will fail to recognize the strength and even magnificence of particular sections: the record of the visionary experience in section XCV, for example, the moving simplicity of section XIX, and the concentrated force of section VII. For some modern readers and critics, in short, *In Memoriam* does continue to live, in parts if not as a whole, and some words of Basil Willey's are eloquent testimony to the fact:

[In *In Memoriam*] Tennyson's lyric power, the greatest of his gifts, was allowed full play, and we get therefore something very unusual: a long poem free from epic pomp, and built up, like a coral-reef, entirely from living organisms. Moreover, in this poem we find all Tennyson's distinctive graces in fragrant blow together. His artistry is at its height, every verse and line being wrought as near perfection as he could make it; yet such is the pressure of emotion, so compelling the need for utterance, that artificiality is avoided. Similarly, *In Memoriam* is the richest of all repositories of the five-word jewels, exquisite landscapes, renderings of the shifting panorama of the seasons; but these are employed as vehicles and symbols of the poet's changing moods and share in his imaginative life. They never strike us . . . as decoration mechanically and coldly applied from without.[2]

Apart from his dramas, which fall outside the scope of this essay, the major achievement of Tennyson's later years was

---

[1] Baum, op. cit., p. 130.
[2] Basil Willey, *More Nineteenth Century Studies*, London, 1956, p. 90.

The Idylls of the King. The final publication of the completed *Idylls* in twelve books did not come until 1888, but this was the culmination of a complicated series of previous publications and of Tennyson's long-standing obsession with the Arthurian story, of which the earliest published evidence is the first version of 'The Lady of Shalott' in the 1832 volume. His source for this early poem seems not to have been Malory but an Italian romance from a collection called *Cento Novelle Antiche*; later he used Malory's version of the same legendary episode as the basis of 'Lancelot and Elaine', one of the most successful of the *Idylls* proper. The greatest of the twelve books, 'The Passing of Arthur'—which is included in this selection and which incorporates the 'Morte d'Arthur' from the 1842 edition—is not itself an 'idyll' but in the nature of an end-piece, the counterpart of the opening section, 'The Coming of Arthur'.

There has been much discussion of the meaning of the *Idylls.* Tennyson himself admitted that 'there is an allegorical or perhaps rather a parabolic drift in the poems',[1] but he also declared that 'there is no single fact or incident in the "Idylls", however seemingly mystical, which cannot be explained as without any mystery or allegory whatever'.[2] Hallam Tennyson records:

The Bishop of Ripon (Boyd Carpenter) once asked him whether they were right who interpreted the three Queens, who accompanied King Arthur on his last voyage, as Faith, Hope and Charity. He answered: 'They are right, and they are not right. They mean that and they do not. They are three of the noblest of women. They are also those three Graces, but they are much more. I hate to be tied down to say, '*This* means *that*,' because the thought within the image is much more than any one interpretation.[3]

[1] *Memoir*, ii. 127.   [2] Ibid.
[3] Ibid.

We have some clues, however, to the 'parabolic drift' of the *Idylls*. In his first notes for the poem Tennyson identified Arthur with religious faith, Modred with 'the sceptical understanding', and the Round Table with 'liberal institutions'.[1] Later he declared that Arthur represented the soul, and Hallam Tennyson, again, tells us that the unity of the *Idylls* is related to 'the unending war of humanity in all ages,—the world-wide war of Sense and Soul, typified in individuals, with the subtle interaction of character upon character, the central dominant figure being the pure, generous, tender, brave, human-hearted Arthur'.[2] Working from such hints F. E. L. Priestley develops an enthusiastic defence of the much-criticized *Idylls* as 'one of Tennyson's most earnest and important efforts to deal with major problems of his time'.[3] He concludes:

The *Idylls* present in allegory the philosophy which pervades the whole of Tennyson's poetry, the philosophy which he felt it necessary to assert throughout his poetic lifetime. Penetrating all his poetry is the strong faith in the eternal world of spirit. . . . The assertion of the validity and necessity of idealism is reinforced by continual warnings of the dangers of materialism. . . . Tennyson is asserting in the *Idylls* that Christianity is not so much a set of facts to be argued about as a system of principles to be lived by; that the proof of these principles is to be established not by external empirical evidence, but by the power with which they unify and give stability and meaning to the life of man and of societies. He wants to make the reader understand how these principles become neglected, and what must happen to individuals and societies who neglect them. He is voicing a warning to his own age and nation, and to all ages and nations.[4]

Modern criticism has not often viewed the *Idylls* in such a favourable light. Harold Nicolson felt that the *Idylls*, along

---

[1] *Memoir*, ii. 123.   [2] Ibid., ii. 130.
[3] F. E. L. Priestley, 'Tennyson's Idylls', in John Killham (ed.), *Critical Essays on the Poetry of Tennyson*, London, 1960, p. 239. First published in *University of Toronto Quarterly*, xix (1949).   [4] Ibid., pp. 254–5.

with the *Enoch Arden* volume of 1864 and other poems of 'the Farringford period', fell under suspicion of intellectual insincerity, with the result that the reaction of modern readers was bound to be one of 'estrangement and hostility'.[1] Yet even Nicolson acknowledges that the *Idylls* contain passages of excellent poetry and that 'The Passing of Arthur', in particular, is 'a magnificent poem, magnificently treated'.[2] And, whatever our reaction to the overall achievement and obscure 'message' of the *Idylls*, there can be no doubt of the effectiveness of Tennyson's description of that 'last weird battle in the west', with its mingled unreality and horror, its disturbing 'wasteland' imagery (see especially lines 81–98).

Passing over the period when Tennyson was mainly occupied with the writing of his plays, we come to what Nicolson calls 'the splendid Aldworth period', which he dates from 1880. It is always dangerous to make sweeping generalizations about Tennyson, as Nicolson's blanket condemnation of the 'Farringford period' clearly shows, but these final years undoubtedly saw the production of some very remarkable poetry indeed. 'Rizpah', for example, written when Tennyson was seventy-two, is greatly superior to most of the earlier 'English Idyls' and other domestic narratives, such as 'Aylmer's Field' and 'Enoch Arden', which were so popular in Tennyson's own lifetime. Stopford A. Brooke's comparison of 'Rizpah' to *King Lear* carried appreciative criticism too far—'Rizpah' is nearer to the best of Crabbe than it is to Shakespeare—but Brooke was obviously right in seizing on the starkness and horror of the poem.[3] A reading of 'Rizpah' reminds us that Tennyson, even in his last years, cannot be summed up in any single, comfortable, all-embracing formula. In these years, for

[1] Nicolson, op. cit., p. 231.   [2] Ibid.
[3] Stopford A. Brooke, *Tennyson: His Art and Relation to Modern Life*, London, 1894, p. 424.

example, he wrote 'Vastness', with its mood of profound disturbance, and 'Crossing the Bar', with its mood of clear serenity. And alongside the wildness of 'Rizpah' we must put the supreme orderliness of 'Frater Ave Atque Vale' and 'To Virgil'. 'Frater Ave Atque Vale', written during a visit to Italy in the summer of 1880, combines Tennyson's regret at the death the previous year of his brother Charles with a gracious compliment to the Latin poet Catullus, and to Catullus's elegy for his own brother, and the poem is as moving as it is skilful (see Nicolson's analysis of Tennyson's manipulation of the vowel patterns).[1] 'To Virgil' is an 'occasional' poem, written for the nineteenth centenary of Virgil's death in 1882, but its strength derives in large measure from Tennyson's deep sympathy with his subject. As Douglas Bush observes, 'To Virgil' is 'the briefest and finest appreciation of Virgil ever written',[2] and what the poem very plainly demonstrates is that Tennyson was a master of dignified, often stately compliment.

The supreme instance of this mastery had appeared many years before. His 'Ode on the Death of the Duke of Wellington', written in 1852, is not only a model of its kind but ranks with Milton's 'Lycidas' and Shelley's 'Adonais' among the great elegies of the English language. Despite the apparent irregularity of metre and rhyme, the form of the 'Ode' is firm, and precisely integrated with the subject. The shape of the poem is moulded to the progress of the funeral procession and service, with the attendant rituals of the tolling of bells and the firing of cannon, and its unity is further strengthened by the patterning of sound and rhythm achieved especially by the constant recurrence of particular sounds, words, and even whole lines. Tennyson is perhaps most consistently at his best

---

[1] Nicolson, op. cit., pp. 285–6.
[2] Douglas Bush, *Mythology and the Romantic Tradition in English Poetry*, Cambridge, Mass., 1937, p. 226.

in the elegiac mood, which dominates not only the Wellington 'Ode' and the best sections of *In Memoriam* but also 'Frater Ave Atque Vale', 'The Garden at Swainston', and the lines, delicately combining gracious compliment with deeply felt personal emotion, with which he dedicated the very late volume, *Demeter and Other Poems*, to Lord Dufferin. Many of the qualities which distinguish his elegies appear also, though at a lower intensity, in his official, Laureate poems. Fortified by his classical training, well supplied with models, his 'fine ear' representing for once a strictly relevant skill, Tennyson was able to deal competently and even triumphantly with the demands for poems on royal births, marriages, and deaths, on battles, exhibitions, and jubilees, to which his Laureateship exposed him. The Laureateship may have been occupied by greater poets than Tennyson—Wordsworth is the outstanding example—but none of them discharged the office itself with more consistent success.

Although it is not for his Laureate poems, apart from the Wellington 'Ode', that we now read Tennyson, the same qualities which made him such a successful Laureate also give strength to the poems by which he now lives, and will continue to live. There has been little discussion in this essay of Tennyson's various technical excellences, the much-praised 'fine ear', the mellifluousness and the 'vowel-music', the 'word-pictures' and the mastery of figurative devices. These qualities, though admirable enough, are not in themselves guarantees of poetic greatness; they are also qualities which the reader readily perceives for himself and which have been extensively discussed elsewhere. Indeed, it is all too easy to distinguish and illustrate these qualities without carrying the discussion of Tennyson any further. His most fervent admirers in this century have praised him as a musician, as a landscape-painter, as a creator of moods, occasionally as a visionary.

They have felt unable to defend him as a philosopher and as a prophet; and, indeed, it seems unlikely that any future generation will be able to think of Tennyson as his contemporaries thought of him—as a great thinker, as seer and sage.

Yet Tennyson is far from being, as W. H. Auden claimed, 'undoubtedly the stupidest' of the English poets.[1] He was not a systematic thinker, but he thought long and deeply about the problems of his own age, especially those which he experienced personally in terms of his own griefs, joys, doubts, and convictions. Tennyson did not 'surrender' to his age, any more than he deliberately sought the prophetic role in which his contemporaries cast him. He wrote of his age because of his own intimate participation in its anxieties, which comprised, indeed, a very large segment of his experience. There can be no doubt that Tennyson suffered as a poet, and especially in his later years, as a result of the severe limitations of the life he led. His very emotions, apart from the one great event of Hallam's death, seem to have been largely literary, aroused by books rather than by actual living, and it was natural, therefore, that he should find himself returning again and again, in his desperate search for a poetic 'subject', to the same group of general and abstract ideas—ideas which he was intellectually ill-equipped to handle, but whose agonizing relevance for himself and, by natural extension, his contemporaries he could all too clearly recognize.

If Tennyson did arrive at a compromise with his age, it was not the compromise of which so many critics have written and by which he is supposed to have sold his poetic birthright in return for the assurance of contemporary fame and affluence. Tennyson's compromise was one which allowed him to combine the two often contradictory duties which he believed to

[1] W. H. Auden (ed.), *Tennyson: An Introduction and a Selection*, London, 1946, p. x.

lie upon him. One of these was to speak words of comfort to his troubled age—and to his grieving queen: there can be no doubt that Tennyson was deeply affected by his personal relationship with Queen Victoria and his respect for her suffering. The other duty was to speak truth, to give honest testimony. The compromise took the form, almost inevitably, of indirection. Certain aspects of Tennyson's vision, it would seem, were too dark, too despairing, too anarchical, to be directly uttered. It is perhaps for this reason that he resorted, in such poems as 'Locksley Hall', *Maud*, and even 'Rizpah', to the use of a mentally unstable narrator, a device which allowed the statements of the poems to be disowned by the poet but at the same time to receive some ratification from the very force of the language in which they were conveyed. This may also be the source of the ambivalence of the *Idylls*; for, whatever interpretation may be given to the shadowy allegory, there can be no doubt that the surface events of the poem display, as Stopford A. Brooke was horrified to discern,

not only the partial failure of purity of life . . . [but] its complete over-throw. . . . Not a soul keeps the vows, except Arthur and those who have left the world for the cloister. I do not understand why [Tennyson] works out a result which seems not only to contradict the possibility of his rule of chastity being observed, but which makes that rule issue in a wholly shameless society. It is as if he despaired of purity. The thing he most insists on is made by him to be the impossible thing. This is an excessively curious conclusion for Tennyson to come to.[1]

Brooke is frank in his bewilderment. Many of Tennyson's other admirers have tended to avoid such difficulties. T. S. Eliot, however, noted that the expression of doubt in *In Memoriam* was more convincing than the expression of faith,

[1] Stopford A. Brooke, op. cit., pp. 363–4.

and more recently Jerome H. Buckley, Arthur J. Carr, in his article on 'Tennyson as a Modern Poet',[1] and, above all, E. D. H. Johnson, in his study entitled *The Alien Vision of Victorian Poetry*, have all confronted, to a greater or lesser degree, the problems posed by the ambiguities and contradictions of Tennyson's later poetry. It is difficult to accept all of Johnson's conclusions about individual poems—he seems too much concerned with Tennyson's aesthetic philosophy and too little with his social and religious views—but he is surely right in his central argument that Tennyson was often fundamentally at odds with the official values of his day, and that he continued to the end of his life to express his 'private insights' even while framing his work to meet the requirements of a popular audience. 'Beneath his artistic productivity,' writes Johnson, 'lay dark depths of consciousness on communion with which, rather than on any external stimulus, depended his will to create.'[2] Tennyson was certainly not insensitive to the pressures exerted by contemporary society:

Yet there are evidences enough that, even during the years of his greatest prestige as Victorian man of letters, Tennyson held aloof from his age and continued to live most intensely within the world of his own mind. Since, however, the conscious artist took pains to sublimate any traces of his inner consciousness, the revelations of its operation must be sought not on the surface of his poetry, but rather in the modes of perception by which he illuminated subject-matter ostensibly selected for its popular appeal. The thoughtful reader, who approaches the poetry of the 1850's and 1860's by way of what came before, can hardly fail to observe in this later work the recurrence of certain themes and an habitual reliance on certain formal devices [Johnson examines Tennyson's use of madness, dreams, and visions]

---

[1] In John Killham (ed.), *Critical Essays on the Poetry of Tennyson*, pp. 41–64. First published in *University of Toronto Quarterly*, xix (1950).

[2] E. D. H. Johnson, *The Alien Vision of Victorian Poetry*, Princeton, 1952, p. 66.

which are at variance with the expressed content of the material. It is as though there brooded in the background a mind constantly alert to strange and disturbing implications in the most commonplace circumstances. Thus, many of the poems which seem to be indisputably the products of Victorian literary convention have an extra dimension which, once recognized, relates them to the deeper sources of the author's poetic vision.[1]

We are still, perhaps, too close to Tennyson to be able to arrive at a just estimation of his stature as a poet. His death was an event within the memory of many people now living, and only now, as the denigrators of Victorianism are themselves falling out of favour, can we begin to see him in proper perspective. For the modern poet, it is true, Tennyson is still not a contemporary, a living force. But Tennyson has never ceased to be widely read, quoted, and admired, his poems have always had a steady sale, and in recent years critical appreciation of his work has been steadily growing. T. S. Eliot is firm in his judgement: 'Tennyson is a great poet, for reasons that are perfectly clear. He has three qualities which are seldom found together except in the greatest poets: abundance, variety, and complete competence.'[2] Tennyson did not produce any monumental work of genius such as *Paradise Lost*; he has not given the world a new vision of itself as Wordsworth did; he may even have written nothing quite so indispensable in the English poetic tradition as two or three pieces by Marvell. Yet the abundance, the variety, and the competence, the superlative technical excellence, are indisputable, and Tennyson's essential greatness cannot be denied.

[1] Ibid., p. 22.   [2] Eliot, op. cit., p. 328.

TENNYSON'S LIFE

1809 Born at Somersby, Lincolnshire, on August 6th.

1815–20 At Louth Grammar School.

1826 *Poems by Two Brothers* published by Jacksons of Louth.

1828–31 At Trinity College, Cambridge.

1829 Awarded Chancellor's Medal for the prize poem *Timbuctoo*.

1830 Spring. First meeting with Emily Sellwood.
June. Publication of *Poems, Chiefly Lyrical*.
July–September. Tennyson and Arthur Hallam visit the Pyrenees with money and instructions for the Spanish revolutionaries.

1831 January (?). Hallam becomes engaged to Tennyson's sister Emily.
March. Death of Tennyson's father. Tennyson leaves Cambridge without taking a degree.

1832 May. Review of *Poems, Chiefly Lyrical* by 'Christopher North' (Professor John Wilson) in *Blackwood's Magazine*.
December. Publication of *Poems* (date on title-page is 1833).

1833 April. Review of *Poems* by John Wilson Croker in the *Quarterly Review*.
15 September. Sudden death of Arthur Hallam in Vienna.

1836 May. Emily Sellwood acts as bridesmaid at the marriage of her sister Louisa to Tennyson's brother Charles.

1837 Tennyson family moves from Somersby to High Beech, near Epping, Essex.

1838 Tennyson formally engaged to Emily Sellwood.

1840 Engagement broken off.
Tennyson family moves to Tunbridge Wells, Kent.

1841 Tennyson family moves again to Boxley, near Maidstone, Kent. Nearby was Park House, home of the Lushingtons and later the setting for *The Princess*.

1842 May. *Poems* published, in two volumes; also published in America by Ticknor.

1843 Tennyson loses his capital in failure of Dr. Allen's scheme for wood-carving by machinery.

1844 Tennyson family moves to Cheltenham. Tennyson undergoes treatment in a hydropathic hospital nearby.

1845 Sir Robert Peel, the Prime Minister, secures Tennyson a Civil List
       pension of £200 a year.

1847 November. Publication of *The Princess* (six songs added in 3rd
       edn., 1850).

1850 Spring. Tennyson and Emily Sellwood meet again and their en-
       gagement is renewed.
       1 June. Publication of *In Memoriam*, anonymously at first.
       13 June. Marriage to Emily Sellwood.
       November. Tennyson made Poet Laureate.

1851 Tennyson and his wife move into Chapel House, Twickenham.

1852 August. Birth of Hallam Tennyson.
       November. Publication of the *Ode on the Death of the Duke of
       Wellington*.

1853 November. Tennyson moves to Farringford, near Freshwater,
       Isle of Wight.

1854 March. Birth of Lionel Tennyson.
       December. 'The Charge of the Light Brigade' published.

1855 July. Publication of *Maud, and Other Poems*.

1859 June. Publication of the *Idylls of the King*, containing 'Enid',
       'Vivien', 'Elaine', and 'Guinevere'.

1864 July. Publication of *Enoch Arden and Other Poems*.

1865 February. Death of Tennyson's mother.

1867 Building of Aldworth (near Haslemere, Surrey) begun.

1869 December. Publication of *The Holy Grail, and Other Poems* (date
       on title-page 1870).

1871 December. 'The Last Tournament' published in the *Contemporary
       Review*.

1872 Publication of *Gareth and Lynette* volume.
       Idylls published in sequence in the Library Edition of Tenny-
       son's works.

1874 September. Emily Tennyson falls ill. Hallam leaves Cambridge to
       be his father's secretary.

1875 May. Publication of *Queen Mary* (play).

1876 March–April. *Queen Mary* runs for five weeks at the Lyceum
       Theatre with Henry Irving as Philip II of Spain.
       November. Publication of *Harold* (play).

1879 Publication of *The Lover's Tale* (first authorized edition of this
       early poem).

1880 November. Publication of *Ballads and Other Poems*.

1883 Tennyson accepts a barony.

1884 Publication of *Becket* (play: successfully produced by Irving in 1893).

Publication of *The Cup* and *The Falcon* (plays: the former had been produced in 1881, the latter in 1879).

1885 Publication of *Tiresias and Other Poems*.

1886 Death of Lionel Tennyson on his way home from India.

Publication of *Locksley Hall Sixty Years After, Etc.*

1888–9 Tennyson has a severe attack of rheumatic gout.

1889 Publication of *Demeter and Other Poems*.

1892 Publication of *The Foresters: Robin Hood and Maid Marian* (play: successfully performed in New York in March 1892).

6 October. Tennyson dies at Aldworth. Buried in Westminster Abbey.

Publication of *The Death of Oenone, Akbar's Dream, and Other Poems*.

SELECT BIBLIOGRAPHY

I. EDITIONS OF TENNYSON'S WORKS

(a) *Collected Works*

Works. Eversley edition. Annotated by Alfred, Lord Tennyson; edited by Hallam, Lord Tennyson (London, 1907–8, 9 vols.). The standard text.

Poetical Works, including the Plays. Oxford Standard Authors (London, 1953). The best text in print.

(b) *Selections and Separate Works*

The Devil and the Lady. Edited by Sir Charles Tennyson (London, 1930).

Unpublished Early Poems. Edited by Sir Charles Tennyson (London, 1931).

II. BIOGRAPHY AND CRITICISM

(a) *Books*

Hallam, Lord Tennyson. *Alfred Lord Tennyson: A Memoir* (London, 1897, 2 vols.; 1899 in one vol.). A rich source-book for the study of Tennyson's life and work.

Harold Nicolson. *Tennyson: Aspects of his Life, Character and Poetry* (London, 1923. Paperback edn., 1960). The starting-point of modern Tennyson criticism.

Paull F. Baum. *Tennyson Sixty Years After* (Chapel Hill, North Carolina, 1948). Rather hostile interpretation with interesting analyses of particular poems.

Sir Charles Tennyson. *Alfred Tennyson* (London, 1949). The standard biography.

Edgar F. Shannon, Jr. *Tennyson and the Reviewers* (Cambridge, Mass., 1952). A study of Tennyson's early critics and their influence on his work.

E. D. H. Johnson. *The Alien Vision of Victorian Poetry* (Princeton, 1952). Argues that Tennyson, like Arnold and Browning, was often fundamentally in conflict with the age in which he lived.

F. L. Lucas. *Tennyson* (London, 1957). Brief study and helpful bibliography.

John Killham, ed. *Critical Essays on the Poetry of Tennyson* (London, 1960). Very useful collection of modern essays, with a review of modern criticism by the editor.

Jerome Hamilton Buckley. *Tennyson: The Growth of a Poet* (Cambridge, Mass., and London, 1960). A sympathetic study and the first to make use of the unpublished Tennyson Papers at Harvard.

Valerie Pitt. *Tennyson Laureate* (London, 1962). A recent study containing interesting material.

(b) *Articles*

F. L. Lucas, 'Tennyson', in *Eight Victorian Poets* (Cambridge, 1930). Later republished as *Ten Victorian Poets*, 1940. Short, appreciative chapter praising Tennyson as landscape-painter and musician.

T. S. Eliot, '*In Memoriam*', in *Essays Ancient and Modern* (London, 1936). Repr. in *Selected Essays*, 3rd edn., 1951, and in Killham, ed., *Critical Essays*. Important evaluation of *In Memoriam* and of Tennyson's whole achievement.

Douglas Bush, 'Tennyson', in *Mythology and the Romantic Tradition in English Poetry* (Cambridge, Mass., 1937). Chapter on Tennyson's use of classical materials.

G. M. Young, 'The Age of Tennyson', in *Today and Yesterday* (London, 1948). Repr. in Killham, ed., *Critical Essays*. Brief, witty account of Tennyson in relation to his times.

Arthur J. Carr, 'Tennyson as a Modern Poet', *University of Toronto Quarterly*, xix (1950), 361–82. Repr. in Killham, ed., *Critical Essays*. Perceptive and provocative essay.

Humphry House, 'Tennyson and the Spirit of the Age' and '*In Memoriam*', in *All in Due Time* (London, 1955). Brief but helpful essays.

Paull F. Baum, 'Alfred Lord Tennyson', in Frederic E. Faverty, ed., *The Victorian Poets: A Guide to Research* (Cambridge, Mass., 1956). Survey of Tennyson criticism and scholarship.

NOTE ON THE TEXT

THE text throughout is that of the Eversley edition of 1907–8; in seven instances of obviously defective punctuation emended readings have been silently adopted from the one-volume Complete Edition of 1894.

THE POEMS

Claribel

A MELODY

Poems, Chiefly Lyrical (1830)

I

WHERE Claribel low-lieth
  The breezes pause and die,
    Letting the rose-leaves fall:
But the solemn oak-tree sigheth,
  Thick-leaved, ambrosial,   5
  With an ancient melody
  Of an inward agony,
Where Claribel low-lieth.

II

At eve the beetle boometh
  Athwart the thicket lone: 10
At noon the wild bee hummeth
  About the moss'd headstone:
At midnight the moon cometh,
  And looketh down alone.
Her song the lintwhite swelleth,   15
The clear-voiced mavis dwelleth,
  The callow throstle lispeth,
The slumbrous wave outwelleth,
  The babbling runnel crispeth,
The hollow grot replieth   20
  Where Claribel low-lieth.

Mariana

Poems, Chiefly Lyrical (1830)

'Mariana in the moated grange.'
Measure for Measure

WITH blackest moss the flower-plots
  Were thickly crusted, one and all:
The rusted nails fell from the knots
  That held the pear to the gable-wall.
The broken sheds look'd sad and strange: 5
  Unlifted was the clinking latch;
  Weeded and worn the ancient thatch
Upon the lonely moated grange.
    She only said, 'My life is dreary,
      He cometh not,' she said;   10
    She said, 'I am aweary, aweary,
      I would that I were dead!'

Her tears fell with the dews at even;
  Her tears fell ere the dews were dried;
She could not look on the sweet heaven,   15
  Either at morn or eventide.
After the flitting of the bats,
  When thickest dark did trance the sky,
  She drew her casement-curtain by,
And glanced athwart the glooming flats.   20
    She only said, 'The night is dreary,
      He cometh not,' she said;
    She said, 'I am aweary, aweary,
      I would that I were dead!'

Upon the middle of the night,   25
   Waking she heard the night-fowl crow:
The cock sung out an hour ere light:
   From the dark fen the oxen's low
Came to her: without hope of change,
   In sleep she seem'd to walk forlorn,   30
   Till cold winds woke the gray-eyed morn
About the lonely moated grange.
     She only said, 'The day is dreary,
       He cometh not,' she said;
     She said, 'I am aweary, aweary,   35
       I would that I were dead!'

About a stone-cast from the wall
   A sluice with blacken'd waters slept,
And o'er it many, round and small,
   The cluster'd marish-mosses crept.   40
Hard by a poplar shook alway,
   All silver-green with gnarled bark:
   For leagues no other tree did mark
The level waste, the rounding gray.
     She only said, 'My life is dreary,   45
       He cometh not,' she said;
     She said, 'I am aweary, aweary,
       I would that I were dead!'

And ever when the moon was low,
   And the shrill winds were up and away,   50
In the white curtain, to and fro,
   She saw the gusty shadow sway.
But when the moon was very low,
   And wild winds bound within their cell,
   The shadow of the poplar fell   55
Upon her bed, across her brow.

She only said, 'The night is dreary,
    He cometh not,' she said;
She said, 'I am aweary, aweary,
    I would that I were dead!'   60

All day within the dreamy house,
    The doors upon their hinges creak'd;
The blue fly sung in the pane; the mouse
    Behind the mouldering wainscot shriek'd,
Or from the crevice peer'd about.   65
    Old faces glimmer'd thro' the doors,
    Old footsteps trod the upper floors,
Old voices called her from without.
    She only said, 'My life is dreary,
        He cometh not,' she said;   70
    She said, 'I am aweary, aweary,
        I would that I were dead!'

The sparrow's chirrup on the roof,
    The slow clock ticking, and the sound
Which to the wooing wind aloof   75
    The poplar made, did all confound
Her sense; but most she loathed the hour
    When the thick-moted sunbeam lay
    Athwart the chambers, and the day
Was sloping toward his western bower.   80
    Then, said she, 'I am very dreary,
        He will not come,' she said;
    She wept, 'I am aweary, aweary,
        Oh God, that I were dead!'

The Dying Swan

Poems, Chiefly Lyrical (1830)

I

THE plain was grassy, wild and bare,
Wide, wild, and open to the air,
Which had built up everywhere
   An under-roof of doleful gray.
With an inner voice the river ran,   5
Adown it floated a dying swan,
     And loudly did lament.
   It was the middle of the day.
Ever the weary wind went on,
     And took the reed-tops as it went.   10

II

Some blue peaks in the distance rose,
And white against the cold-white sky,
Shone out their crowning snows.
   One willow over the river wept,
And shook the wave as the wind did sigh;   15
Above in the wind was the swallow,
     Chasing itself at its own wild will,
     And far thro' the marish green and still
     The tangled water-courses slept,
Shot over with purple, and green, and yellow.   20

III

The wild swan's death-hymn took the soul
Of that waste place with joy
Hidden in sorrow: at first to the ear
The warble was low, and full and clear;

And floating about the under-sky, 25
Prevailing in weakness, the coronach stole
Sometimes afar, and sometimes anear;
But anon her awful jubilant voice,
With a music strange and manifold,
Flow'd forth on a carol free and bold; 30
As when a mighty people rejoice
With shawms, and with cymbals, and harps of gold,
And the tumult of their acclaim is roll'd
Thro' the open gates of the city afar,
To the shepherd who watcheth the evening star. 35
And the creeping mosses and clambering weeds,
And the willow-branches hoar and dank,
And the wavy swell of the soughing reeds,
And the wave-worn horns of the echoing bank,
And the silvery marish-flowers that throng 40
The desolate creeks and pools among,
Were flooded over with eddying song.

Fatima

Poems (1832: 1833 on title-page)

O Love, Love, Love! O withering might!
O sun, that from thy noonday height
Shudderest when I strain my sight,
Throbbing thro' all thy heat and light,
    Lo, falling from my constant mind, 5
    Lo, parch'd and wither'd, deaf and blind,
    I whirl like leaves in roaring wind.

Last night I wasted hateful hours
Below the city's eastern towers:

I thirsted for the brooks, the showers: 10
I roll'd among the tender flowers:
  I crush'd them on my breast, my mouth;
  I look'd athwart the burning drouth
  Of that long desert to the south.

Last night, when some one spoke his name,   15
From my swift blood that went and came
A thousand little shafts of flame
Were shiver'd in my narrow frame.
  O Love, O fire! once he drew
  With one long kiss my whole soul thro'   20
  My lips, as sunlight drinketh dew.

Before he mounts the hill, I know
He cometh quickly: from below
Sweet gales, as from deep gardens, blow
Before him, striking on my brow.   25
  In my dry brain my spirit soon,
  Down-deepening from swoon to swoon,
  Faints like a dazzled morning moon.

The wind sounds like a silver wire,
And from beyond the noon a fire   30
Is pour'd upon the hills, and nigher
The skies stoop down in their desire;
  And, isled in sudden seas of light,
  My heart, pierced thro' with fierce delight,
  Bursts into blossom in his sight.   35

My whole soul waiting silently,
All naked in a sultry sky,
Droops blinded with his shining eye:
I *will* possess him or will die.

I will grow round him in his place,   40
Grow, live, die looking on his face,
Die, dying clasp'd in his embrace.

The Lady of Shalott

Poems (1842); earlier version in *Poems* (1832)

PART I

ON either side the river lie
Long fields of barley and of rye,
That clothe the wold and meet the sky;
And thro' the field the road runs by
  To many-tower'd Camelot;   5
And up and down the people go,
Gazing where the lilies blow
Round an island there below,
  The island of Shalott.

Willows whiten, aspens quiver,   10
Little breezes dusk and shiver
Thro' the wave that runs for ever
By the island in the river
  Flowing down to Camelot.
Four gray walls, and four gray towers,   15
Overlook a space of flowers,
And the silent isle imbowers
  The Lady of Shalott.

By the margin, willow-veil'd,
Slide the heavy barges trail'd   20
By slow horses; and unhail'd
The shallop flitteth silken-sail'd
  Skimming down to Camelot:

But who hath seen her wave her hand?
Or at the casement seen her stand?   25
Or is she known in all the land,
    The Lady of Shalott?

Only reapers, reaping early
In among the bearded barley,
Hear a song that echoes cheerly   30
From the river winding clearly,
    Down to tower'd Camelot:
And by the moon the reaper weary,
Piling sheaves in uplands airy,
Listening, whispers "Tis the fairy   35
    Lady of Shalott.'

PART II

THERE she weaves by night and day
A magic web with colours gay.
She has heard a whisper say,
A curse is on her if she stay   40
    To look down to Camelot.
She knows not what the curse may be,
And so she weaveth steadily,
And little other care hath she,
    The Lady of Shalott.   45

And moving thro' a mirror clear
That hangs before her all the year,
Shadows of the world appear.
There she sees the highway near
    Winding down to Camelot: 50

There the river eddy whirls,
And there the surly village-churls,
And the red cloaks of market girls,
    Pass onward from Shalott.

Sometimes a troop of damsels glad,   55
An abbot on an ambling pad,
Sometimes a curly shepherd-lad,
Or long-hair'd page in crimson clad,
    Goes by to tower'd Camelot;
And sometimes thro' the mirror blue   60
The knights come riding two and two:
She hath no loyal knight and true,
    The Lady of Shalott.

But in her web she still delights
To weave the mirror's magic sights,   65
For often thro' the silent nights
A funeral, with plumes and lights
    And music, went to Camelot:
Or when the moon was overhead,
Came two young lovers lately wed;   70
'I am half sick of shadows,' said
    The Lady of Shalott.

PART III

A BOW-SHOT from her bower-eaves,
He rode between the barley-sheaves,
The sun came dazzling thro' the leaves,   75
And flamed upon the brazen greaves
    Of bold Sir Lancelot.

A red-cross knight for ever kneel'd
To a lady in his shield,
That sparkled on the yellow field,   80
    Beside remote Shalott.

The gemmy bridle glitter'd free,
Like to some branch of stars we see
Hung in the golden Galaxy.
The bridle bells rang merrily   85
    As he rode down to Camelot:
And from his blazon'd baldric slung
A mighty silver bugle hung,
And as he rode his armour rung,
    Beside remote Shalott.   90

All in the blue unclouded weather
Thick-jewell'd shone the saddle-leather,
The helmet and the helmet-feather
Burn'd like one burning flame together,
    As he rode down to Camelot.   95
As often thro' the purple night,
Below the starry clusters bright,
Some bearded meteor, trailing light,
    Moves over still Shalott.

His broad clear brow in sunlight glow'd;   100
On burnish'd hooves his war-horse trode;
From underneath his helmet flow'd
His coal-black curls as on he rode,
    As he rode down to Camelot.
From the bank and from the river   105
He flash'd into the crystal mirror,
'Tirra lirra,' by the river
    Sang Sir Lancelot.

She left the web, she left the loom,
She made three paces thro' the room, 110
She saw the water-lily bloom,
She saw the helmet and the plume,
    She look'd down to Camelot.
Out flew the web and floated wide;
The mirror crack'd from side to side; 115
'The curse is come upon me,' cried
    The Lady of Shalott.

PART IV

In the stormy east-wind straining,
The pale yellow woods were waning,
The broad stream in his banks complaining, 120
Heavily the low sky raining
    Over tower'd Camelot;
Down she came and found a boat
Beneath a willow left afloat,
And round about the prow she wrote 125
    The Lady of Shalott.

And down the river's dim expanse
Like some bold seër in a trance,
Seeing all his own mischance—
With a glassy countenance 130
    Did she look to Camelot.
And at the closing of the day
She loosed the chain, and down she lay;
The broad stream bore her far away,
    The Lady of Shalott. 135

Lying, robed in snowy white
That loosely flew to left and right—

The leaves upon her falling light—
Thro' the noises of the night
    She floated down to Camelot: 140
And as the boat-head wound along
The willowy hills and fields among,
They heard her singing her last song,
    The Lady of Shalott.

Heard a carol, mournful, holy,   145
Chanted loudly, chanted lowly,
Till her blood was frozen slowly,
And her eyes were darken'd wholly,
    Turn'd to tower'd Camelot.
For ere she reach'd upon the tide   150
The first house by the water-side,
Singing in her song she died,
    The Lady of Shalott.

Under tower and balcony,
By garden-wall and gallery,   155
A gleaming shape she floated by,
Dead-pale between the houses high,
    Silent into Camelot.
Out upon the wharfs they came,
Knight and burgher, lord and dame,   160
And round the prow they read her name,
    The Lady of Shalott.

Who is this? and what is here?
And in the lighted palace near
Died the sound of royal cheer;   165
And they cross'd themselves for fear,
    All the knights at Camelot:

But Lancelot mused a little space;
He said, 'She has a lovely face;
God in his mercy lend her grace,   170
    The Lady of Shalott.'

Oenone

Poems (1842); earlier version in Poems (1832)

THERE lies a vale in Ida, lovelier
Than all the valleys of Ionian hills.
The swimming vapour slopes athwart the glen,
Puts forth an arm, and creeps from pine to pine,
And loiters, slowly drawn. On either hand   5
The lawns and meadow-ledges midway down
Hang rich in flowers, and far below them roars
The long brook falling thro' the clov'n ravine
In cataract after cataract to the sea.
Behind the valley topmost Gargarus   10
Stands up and takes the morning: but in front
The gorges, opening wide apart, reveal
Troas and Ilion's column'd citadel,
The crown of Troas.
            Hither came at noon
Mournful Œnone, wandering forlorn   15
Of Paris, once her playmate on the hills.
Her cheek had lost the rose, and round her neck
Floated her hair or seem'd to float in rest.
She, leaning on a fragment twined with vine,
Sang to the stillness, till the mountain-shade   20
Sloped downward to her seat from the upper cliff.

  'O mother Ida, many-fountain'd Ida,
Dear mother Ida, harken ere I die.

For now the noonday quiet holds the hill:
The grasshopper is silent in the grass: 25
The lizard, with his shadow on the stone,
Rests like a shadow, and the winds are dead.
The purple flower droops: the golden bee
Is lily-cradled: I alone awake.
My eyes are full of tears, my heart of love, 30
My heart is breaking, and my eyes are dim,
And I am all aweary of my life.

'O mother Ida, many-fountain'd Ida,
Dear mother Ida, harken ere I die.
Hear me, O Earth, hear me, O Hills, O Caves 35
That house the cold crown'd snake! O mountain brooks,
I am the daughter of a River-God,
Hear me, for I will speak, and build up all
My sorrow with my song, as yonder walls
Rose slowly to a music slowly breathed, 40
A cloud that gather'd shape: for it may be
That, while I speak of it, a little while
My heart may wander from its deeper woe.

'O mother Ida, many-fountain'd Ida,
Dear mother Ida, harken ere I die. 45
I waited underneath the dawning hills,
Aloft the mountain lawn was dewy-dark,
And dewy dark aloft the mountain pine:
Beautiful Paris, evil-hearted Paris,
Leading a jet-black goat white-horn'd, white-hooved, 50
Came up from reedy Simois all alone.

'O mother Ida, harken ere I die.
Far-off the torrent call'd me from the cleft:
Far up the solitary morning smote

The streaks of virgin snow. With down-dropt eyes   55
I sat alone: white-breasted like a star
Fronting the dawn he moved; a leopard skin
Droop'd from his shoulder, but his sunny hair
Cluster'd about his temples like a God's:
And his cheek brighten'd as the foam-bow brightens   60
When the wind blows the foam, and all my heart
Went forth to embrace him coming ere he came.

'Dear mother Ida, harken ere I die.
He smiled, and opening out his milk-white palm
Disclosed a fruit of pure Hesperian gold,   65
That smelt ambrosially, and while I look'd
And listen'd, the full-flowing river of speech
Came down upon my heart.
                              ' "My own Œnone,
Beautiful-brow'd Œnone, my own soul,
Behold this fruit, whose gleaming rind ingrav'n   70
'For the most fair,' would seem to award it thine,
As lovelier than whatever Oread haunt
The knolls of Ida, loveliest in all grace
Of movement, and the charm of married brows."

'Dear mother Ida, harken ere I die.   75
He prest the blossom of his lips to mine,
And added "This was cast upon the board,
When all the full-faced presence of the Gods
Ranged in the halls of Peleus; whereupon
Rose feud, with question unto whom 'twere due: 80
But light-foot Iris brought it yester-eve,
Delivering, that to me, by common voice
Elected umpire, Herè comes to-day,
Pallas and Aphroditè, claiming each

This meed of fairest. Thou, within the cave   85
Behind yon whispering tuft of oldest pine,
Mayst well behold them unbeheld, unheard
Hear all, and see thy Paris judge of Gods."

'Dear mother Ida, harken ere I die.
It was the deep midnoon: one silvery cloud   90
Had lost his way between the piney sides
Of this long glen. Then to the bower they came,
Naked they came to that smooth-swarded bower,
And at their feet the crocus brake like fire,
Violet, amaracus, and asphodel,   95
Lotos and lilies: and a wind arose,
And overhead the wandering ivy and vine,
This way and that, in many a wild festoon
Ran riot, garlanding the gnarled boughs
With bunch and berry and flower thro' and thro'.   100

'O mother Ida, harken ere I die.
On the tree-tops a crested peacock lit,
And o'er him flow'd a golden cloud, and lean'd
Upon him, slowly dropping fragrant dew.
Then first I heard the voice of her, to whom   105
Coming thro' Heaven, like a light that grows
Larger and clearer, with one mind the Gods
Rise up for reverence. She to Paris made
Proffer of royal power, ample rule
Unquestion'd, overflowing revenue   110
Wherewith to embellish state, "from many a vale
And river-sunder'd champaign clothed with corn,
Or labour'd mine undrainable of ore.
Honour," she said, "and homage, tax and toll,
From many an inland town and haven large,   115

Mast-throng'd beneath her shadowing citadel
In glassy bays among her tallest towers."

'O mother Ida, harken ere I die.
Still she spake on and still she spake of power,
"Which in all action is the end of all;   120
Power fitted to the season; wisdom-bred
And throned of wisdom—from all neighbour crowns
Alliance and allegiance, till thy hand
Fail from the sceptre-staff. Such boon from me,
From me, Heaven's Queen, Paris, to thee king-born,   125
A shepherd all thy life but yet king-born,
Should come most welcome, seeing men, in power
Only, are likest gods, who have attain'd
Rest in a happy place and quiet seats
Above the thunder, with undying bliss   130
In knowledge of their own supremacy."

'Dear mother Ida, harken ere I die.
She ceased, and Paris held the costly fruit
Out at arm's-length, so much the thought of power
Flatter'd his spirit; but Pallas where she stood   135
Somewhat apart, her clear and bared limbs
O'erthwarted with the brazen-headed spear
Upon her pearly shoulder leaning cold,
The while, above, her full and earnest eye
Over her snow-cold breast and angry cheek   140
Kept watch, waiting decision, made reply.

' "Self-reverence, self-knowledge, self-control,
These three alone lead life to sovereign power.
Yet not for power (power of herself
Would come uncall'd for) but to live by law,   145

Acting the law we live by without fear;
And, because right is right, to follow right
Were wisdom in the scorn of consequence."

'Dear mother Ida, harken ere I die.
Again she said: "I woo thee not with gifts.   150
Sequel of guerdon could not alter me
To fairer. Judge thou me by what I am,
So shalt thou find me fairest.
                              Yet, indeed,
If gazing on divinity disrobed
Thy mortal eyes are frail to judge of fair,   155
Unbias'd by self-profit, oh! rest thee sure
That I shall love thee well and cleave to thee,
So that my vigour, wedded to thy blood,
Shall strike within thy pulses, like a God's,
To push thee forward thro' a life of shocks,   160
Dangers, and deeds, until endurance grow
Sinew'd with action, and the full-grown will,
Circled thro' all experiences, pure law,
Commeasure perfect freedom."
                              'Here she ceas'd,
And Paris ponder'd, and I cried, "O Paris,   165
Give it to Pallas!" but he heard me not,
Or hearing would not hear me, woe is me!

'O mother Ida, many-fountain'd Ida,
Dear mother Ida, harken ere I die.
Idalian Aphroditè beautiful,   170
Fresh as the foam, new-bathed in Paphian wells,
With rosy slender fingers backward drew
From her warm brows and bosom her deep hair
Ambrosial, golden round her lucid throat

And shoulder: from the violets her light foot   175
Shone rosy-white, and o'er her rounded form
Between the shadows of the vine-bunches
Floated the glowing sunlights, as she moved.

'Dear mother Ida, harken ere I die.
She with a subtle smile in her mild eyes,   180
The herald of her triumph, drawing nigh
Half-whisper'd in his ear, "I promise thee
The fairest and most loving wife in Greece,"
She spoke and laugh'd: I shut my sight for fear:
But when I look'd, Paris had raised his arm,   185
And I beheld great Herè's angry eyes,
As she withdrew into the golden cloud,
And I was left alone within the bower;
And from that time to this I am alone,
And I shall be alone until I die.   190

'Yet, mother Ida, harken ere I die.
Fairest—why fairest wife? am I not fair?
My love hath told me so a thousand times.
Methinks I must be fair, for yesterday,
When I past by, a wild and wanton pard,   195
Eyed like the evening star, with playful tail
Crouch'd fawning in the weed. Most loving is she?
Ah me, my mountain shepherd, that my arms
Were wound about thee, and my hot lips prest
Close, close to thine in that quick-falling dew   200
Of fruitful kisses, thick as Autumn rains
Flash in the pools of whirling Simois.

'O mother, hear me yet before I die.
They came, they cut away my tallest pines,
My tall dark pines, that plumed the craggy ledge   205

High over the blue gorge, and all between
The snowy peak and snow-white cataract
Foster'd the callow eaglet—from beneath
Whose thick mysterious boughs in the dark morn
The panther's roar came muffled, while I sat   210
Low in the valley. Never, never more
Shall lone Œnone see the morning mist
Sweep thro' them; never see them overlaid
With narrow moon-lit slips of silver cloud,
Between the loud stream and the trembling stars.   215

'O mother, hear me yet before I die.
I wish that somewhere in the ruin'd folds,
Among the fragments tumbled from the glens,
Or the dry thickets, I could meet with her
The Abominable, that uninvited came   220
Into the fair Peleïan banquet-hall,
And cast the golden fruit upon the board,
And bred this change; that I might speak my mind,
And tell her to her face how much I hate
Her presence, hated both of Gods and men.   225

'O mother, hear me yet before I die.
Hath he not sworn his love a thousand times,
In this green valley, under this green hill,
Ev'n on this hand, and sitting on this stone?
Seal'd it with kisses? water'd it with tears?   230
O happy tears, and how unlike to these!
O happy Heaven, how canst thou see my face?
O happy earth, how canst thou bear my weight?
O death, death, death, thou ever-floating cloud,
There are enough unhappy on this earth,   235
Pass by the happy souls, that love to live:

I pray thee, pass before my light of life,
And shadow all my soul, that I may die.
Thou weighest heavy on the heart within,
Weigh heavy on my eyelids: let me die.   240

'O mother, hear me yet before I die.
I will not die alone, for fiery thoughts
Do shape themselves within me, more and more,
Whereof I catch the issue, as I hear
Dead sounds at night come from the inmost hills,   245
Like footsteps upon wool. I dimly see
My far-off doubtful purpose, as a mother
Conjectures of the features of her child
Ere it is born: her child!—a shudder comes
Across me: never child be born of me,   250
Unblest, to vex me with his father's eyes!

'O mother, hear me yet before I die.
Hear me, O earth. I will not die alone,
Lest their shrill happy laughter come to me
Walking the cold and starless road of Death   255
Uncomforted, leaving my ancient love
With the Greek woman. I will rise and go
Down into Troy, and ere the stars come forth
Talk with the wild Cassandra, for she says
A fire dances before her, and a sound   260
Rings ever in her ears of armed men.
What this may be I know not, but I know
That, whereso'er I am by night and day,
All earth and air seem only burning fire.'

The Lotos-Eaters

Poems (1842); earlier version in *Poems* (1832)

'COURAGE!' he said, and pointed toward the land,
'This mounting wave will roll us shoreward soon.'
In the afternoon they came unto a land
In which it seemed always afternoon.
All round the coast the languid air did swoon,   5
Breathing like one that hath a weary dream.
Full-faced above the valley stood the moon;
And like a downward smoke, the slender stream
Along the cliff to fall and pause and fall did seem.

A land of streams! some, like a downward smoke,   10
Slow-dropping veils of thinnest lawn, did go;
And some thro' wavering lights and shadows broke,
Rolling a slumbrous sheet of foam below.
They saw the gleaming river seaward flow
From the inner land: far off, three mountain-tops,   15
Three silent pinnacles of aged snow,
Stood sunset-flush'd: and, dew'd with showery drops,
Up-clomb the shadowy pine above the woven copse.

The charmed sunset linger'd low adown
In the red West: thro' mountain clefts the dale   20
Was seen far inland, and the yellow down
Border'd with palm, and many a winding vale
And meadow, set with slender galingale;
A land where all things always seem'd the same!
And round about the keel with faces pale,   25
Dark faces pale against that rosy flame,
The mild-eyed melancholy Lotos-eaters came.

Branches they bore of that enchanted stem,
Laden with flower and fruit, whereof they gave
To each, but whoso did receive of them,   30
And taste, to him the gushing of the wave
Far far away did seem to mourn and rave
On alien shores; and if his fellow spake,
His voice was thin, as voices from the grave;
And deep-asleep he seem'd, yet all awake,   35
And music in his ears his beating heart did make.

They sat them down upon the yellow sand,
Between the sun and moon upon the shore;
And sweet it was to dream of Fatherland,
Of child, and wife, and slave; but evermore   40
Most weary seem'd the sea, weary the oar,
Weary the wandering fields of barren foam.
Then some one said, 'We will return no more;'
And all at once they sang, 'Our island home
Is far beyond the wave; we will no longer roam.'   45

CHORIC SONG

I

THERE is sweet music here that softer falls
Than petals from blown roses on the grass,
Or night-dews on still waters between walls
Of shadowy granite, in a gleaming pass;
Music that gentlier on the spirit lies,   50
Than tir'd eyelids upon tir'd eyes;
Music that brings sweet sleep down from the blissful skies.
Here are cool mosses deep,
And thro' the moss the ivies creep,
And in the stream the long-leaved flowers weep,   55
And from the craggy ledge the poppy hangs in sleep.

II

Why are we weigh'd upon with heaviness,
And utterly consumed with sharp distress,
While all things else have rest from weariness?
All things have rest: why should we toil alone,   60
We only toil, who are the first of things,
And make perpetual moan,
Still from one sorrow to another thrown:
Nor ever fold our wings,
And cease from wanderings,   65
Nor steep our brows in slumber's holy balm;
Nor harken what the inner spirit sings,
'There is no joy but calm!'
Why should we only toil, the roof and crown of things?

III

Lo! in the middle of the wood,   70
The folded leaf is woo'd from out the bud
With winds upon the branch, and there
Grows green and broad, and takes no care,
Sun-steep'd at noon, and in the moon
Nightly dew-fed; and turning yellow   75
Falls, and floats adown the air.
Lo! sweeten'd with the summer light,
The full-juiced apple, waxing over-mellow,
Drops in a silent autumn night.
All its allotted length of days,   80
The flower ripens in its place,
Ripens and fades, and falls, and hath no toil,
Fast-rooted in the fruitful soil.

IV

Hateful is the dark-blue sky,
Vaulted o'er the dark-blue sea.   85
Death is the end of life; ah, why
Should life all labour be?
Let us alone. Time driveth onward fast,
And in a little while our lips are dumb.
Let us alone. What is it that will last?   90
All things are taken from us, and become
Portions and parcels of the dreadful Past.
Let us alone. What pleasure can we have
To war with evil? Is there any peace
In ever climbing up the climbing wave?   95
All things have rest, and ripen toward the grave
In silence; ripen, fall and cease:
Give us long rest or death, dark death, or dreamful ease.

V

How sweet it were, hearing the downward stream,
With half-shut eyes ever to seem   100
Falling asleep in a half-dream!
To dream and dream, like yonder amber light,
Which will not leave the myrrh-bush on the height;
To hear each other's whisper'd speech;
Eating the Lotos day by day,   105
To watch the crisping ripples on the beach,
And tender curving lines of creamy spray;
To lend our hearts and spirits wholly
To the influence of mild-minded melancholy;
To muse and brood and live again in memory,   110
With those old faces of our infancy

Heap'd over with a mound of grass,
Two handfuls of white dust, shut in an urn of brass!

VI

Dear is the memory of our wedded lives,
And dear the last embraces of our wives   115
And their warm tears: but all hath suffer'd change:
For surely now our household hearths are cold:
Our sons inherit us: our looks are strange:
And we should come like ghosts to trouble joy.
Or else the island princes over-bold   120
Have eat our substance, and the minstrel sings
Before them of the ten years' war in Troy,
And our great deeds, as half-forgotten things.
Is there confusion in the little isle?
Let what is broken so remain.   125
The Gods are hard to reconcile:
'Tis hard to settle order once again.
There *is* confusion worse than death,
Trouble on trouble, pain on pain,
Long labour unto aged breath,   130
Sore task to hearts worn out by many wars
And eyes grown dim with gazing on the pilot-stars.

VII

But, propt on beds of amaranth and moly,
How sweet (while warm airs lull us, blowing lowly)
With half-dropt eyelid still,   135
Beneath a heaven dark and holy,
To watch the long bright river drawing slowly
His waters from the purple hill—

To hear the dewy echoes calling
From cave to cave thro' the thick-twined vine—   140
To watch the emerald-colour'd water falling
Thro' many a wov'n acanthus-wreath divine!
Only to hear and see the far-off sparkling brine,
Only to hear were sweet, stretch'd out beneath the pine.

VIII

The Lotos blooms below the barren peak: 145
The Lotos blows by every winding creek:
All day the wind breathes low with mellower tone:
Thro' every hollow cave and alley lone
Round and round the spicy downs the yellow Lotos-dust is
    blown.
We have had enough of action, and of motion we,   150
Roll'd to starboard, roll'd to larboard, when the surge was
    seething free,
Where the wallowing monster spouted his foam-fountains
    in the sea.
Let us swear an oath, and keep it with an equal mind,
In the hollow Lotos-land to live and lie reclined
On the hills like Gods together, careless of mankind.   155
For they lie beside their nectar, and the bolts are hurl'd
Far below them in the valleys, and the clouds are lightly
    curl'd
Round their golden houses, girdled with the gleaming
    world:
Where they smile in secret, looking over wasted lands,
Blight and famine, plague and earthquake, roaring deeps
    and fiery sands,   160
Clanging fights, and flaming towns, and sinking ships, and
    praying hands.

But they smile, they find a music centred in a doleful song
Steaming up, a lamentation and an ancient tale of wrong,
Like a tale of little meaning tho' the words are strong;
Chanted from an ill-used race of men that cleave the soil, 165
Sow the seed, and reap the harvest with enduring toil,
Storing yearly little dues of wheat, and wine and oil;
Till they perish and they suffer—some, 'tis whisper'd—
    down in hell
Suffer endless anguish, others in Elysian valleys dwell,
Resting weary limbs at last on beds of asphodel. 170
Surely, surely, slumber is more sweet than toil, the shore
Than labour in the deep mid-ocean, wind and wave and oar;
Oh rest ye, brother mariners, we will not wander more.

St. Simeon Stylites

Poems (1842)

ALTHO' I be the basest of mankind,
From scalp to sole one slough and crust of sin,
Unfit for earth, unfit for heaven, scarce meet
For troops of devils, mad with blasphemy,
I will not cease to grasp the hope I hold 5
Of saintdom, and to clamour, mourn and sob,
Battering the gates of heaven with storms of prayer,
Have mercy, Lord, and take away my sin.

    Let this avail, just, dreadful, mighty God,
This not be all in vain, that thrice ten years, 10
Thrice multiplied by superhuman pangs,
In hungers and in thirsts, fevers and cold,
In coughs, aches, stitches, ulcerous throes and cramps,
A sign betwixt the meadow and the cloud,
Patient on this tall pillar I have borne 15

Rain, wind, frost, heat, hail, damp, and sleet, and snow;
And I had hoped that ere this period closed
Thou wouldst have caught me up into thy rest,
Denying not these weather-beaten limbs
The meed of saints, the white robe and the palm.   20
    O take the meaning, Lord: I do not breathe,
Not whisper, any murmur of complaint.
Pain heap'd ten-hundred-fold to this, were still
Less burthen, by ten-hundred-fold, to bear,
Than were those lead-like tons of sin, that crush'd   25
My spirit flat before thee.
                              O Lord, Lord,
Thou knowest I bore this better at the first,
For I was strong and hale of body then;
And tho' my teeth, which now are dropt away,
Would chatter with the cold, and all my beard   30
Was tagg'd with icy fringes in the moon,
I drown'd the whoopings of the owl with sound
Of pious hymns and psalms, and sometimes saw
An angel stand and watch me, as I sang.
Now am I feeble grown; my end draws nigh;   35
I hope my end draws nigh: half deaf I am,
So that I scarce can hear the people hum
About the column's base, and almost blind,
And scarce can recognise the fields I know;
And both my thighs are rotted with the dew;   40
Yet cease I not to clamour and to cry,
While my stiff spine can hold my weary head,
Till all my limbs drop piecemeal from the stone,
Have mercy, mercy: take away my sin.
    O Jesus, if thou wilt not save my soul,   45
Who may be saved? who is it may be saved?
Who may be made a saint, if I fail here?

Show me the man hath suffer'd more than I.
For did not all thy martyrs die one death?
For either they were stoned, or crucified,   50
Or burn'd in fire, or boil'd in oil, or sawn
In twain beneath the ribs; but I die here
To-day, and whole years long, a life of death.
Bear witness, if I could have found a way
(And heedfully I sifted all my thought)   55
More slowly-painful to subdue this home
Of sin, my flesh, which I despise and hate,
I had not stinted practice, O my God.

     For not alone this pillar-punishment,
Not this alone I bore: but while I lived   60
In the white convent down the valley there,
For many weeks about my loins I wore
The rope that haled the buckets from the well,
Twisted as tight as I could knot the noose;
And spake not of it to a single soul,   65
Until the ulcer, eating thro' my skin,
Betray'd my secret penance, so that all
My brethren marvell'd greatly. More than this
I bore, whereof, O God, thou knowest all.

     Three winters, that my soul might grow to thee,   70
I lived up there on yonder mountain side.
My right leg chain'd into the crag, I lay
Pent in a roofless close of ragged stones;
Inswathed sometimes in wandering mist, and twice
Black'd with thy branding thunder, and sometimes   75
Sucking the damps for drink, and eating not,
Except the spare chance-gift of those that came
To touch my body and be heal'd, and live:
And they say then that I work'd miracles,
Whereof my fame is loud amongst mankind,   80

Cured lameness, palsies, cancers. Thou, O God,
Knowest alone whether this was or no.
Have mercy, mercy! cover all my sin.

   Then, that I might be more alone with thee,
Three years I lived upon a pillar, high   85
Six cubits, and three years on one of twelve;
And twice three years I crouch'd on one that rose
Twenty by measure; last of all, I grew
Twice ten long weary weary years to this,
That numbers forty cubits from the soil.   90

   I think that I have borne as much as this—
Or else I dream—and for so long a time,
If I may measure time by yon slow light,
And this high dial, which my sorrow crowns—
So much—even so.

                  And yet I know not well,   95
For that the evil ones come here, and say,
'Fall down, O Simeon: thou hast suffer'd long
For ages and for ages!' then they prate
Of penances I cannot have gone thro',
Perplexing me with lies; and oft I fall,   100
Maybe for months, in such blind lethargies
That Heaven, and Earth, and Time are choked.

                         But yet
Bethink thee, Lord, while thou and all the saints
Enjoy themselves in heaven, and men on earth
House in the shade of comfortable roofs,   105
Sit with their wives by fires, eat wholesome food,
And wear warm clothes, and even beasts have stalls,
I, 'tween the spring and downfall of the light,
Bow down one thousand and two hundred times,
To Christ, the Virgin Mother, and the saints;   110
Or in the night, after a little sleep,

I wake: the chill stars sparkle; I am wet
With drenching dews, or stiff with crackling frost.
I wear an undress'd goatskin on my back;
A grazing iron collar grinds my neck;   115
And in my weak, lean arms I lift the cross,
And strive and wrestle with thee till I die:
O mercy, mercy! wash away my sin.

  O Lord, thou knowest what a man I am;
A sinful man, conceived and born in sin: 120
'Tis their own doing; this is none of mine;
Lay it not to me. Am I to blame for this,
That here come those that worship me? Ha! ha!
They think that I am somewhat. What am I?
The silly people take me for a saint,   125
And bring me offerings of fruit and flowers:
And I, in truth (thou wilt bear witness here)
Have all in all endured as much, and more
Than many just and holy men, whose names
Are register'd and calendar'd for saints.   130

  Good people, you do ill to kneel to me.
What is it I can have done to merit this?
I am a sinner viler than you all.
It may be I have wrought some miracles,
And cured some halt and maim'd; but what of that?   135
It may be, no one, even among the saints,
May match his pains with mine: but what of that?
Yet do not rise; for you may look on me,
And in your looking you may kneel to God.
Speak! is there any of you halt or maim'd?   140
I think you know I have some power with Heaven
From my long penance: let him speak his wish.

  Yes, I can heal him. Power goes forth from me.
They say that they are heal'd. Ah, hark! they shout

'St. Simeon Stylites.' Why, if so,   145
God reaps a harvest in me. O my soul,
God reaps a harvest in thee. If this be,
Can I work miracles and not be saved?
This is not told of any. They were saints.
It cannot be but that I shall be saved;   150
Yea, crown'd a saint. They shout, 'Behold a saint!'
And lower voices saint me from above.
Courage, St. Simeon! This dull chrysalis
Cracks into shining wings, and hope ere death
Spreads more and more and more, that God hath now 155
Sponged and made blank of crimeful record all
My mortal archives.
                        O my sons, my sons,
I, Simeon of the pillar, by surname
Stylites, among men; I, Simeon,
The watcher on the column till the end;   160
I, Simeon, whose brain the sunshine bakes;
I, whose bald brows in silent hours become
Unnaturally hoar with rime, do now
From my high nest of penance here proclaim
That Pontius and Iscariot by my side   165
Show'd like fair seraphs. On the coals I lay,
A vessel full of sin: all hell beneath
Made me boil over. Devils pluck'd my sleeve,
Abaddon and Asmodeus caught at me.
I smote them with the cross; they swarm'd again.   170
In bed like monstrous apes they crush'd my chest:
They flapp'd my light out as I read: I saw
Their faces grow between me and my book;
With colt-like whinny and with hoggish whine
They burst my prayer. Yet this way was left,   175
And by this way I 'scaped them. Mortify

Your flesh, like me, with scourges and with thorns;
Smite, shrink not, spare not. If it may be, fast
Whole Lents, and pray. I hardly, with slow steps,
With slow, faint steps, and much exceeding pain,   180
Have scrambled past those pits of fire, that still
Sing in mine ears. But yield not me the praise:
God only thro' his bounty hath thought fit,
Among the powers and princes of this world,
To make me an example to mankind,   185
Which few can reach to. Yet I do not say
But that a time may come—yea, even now,
Now, now, his footsteps smite the threshold stairs
Of life—I say, that time is at the doors
When you may worship me without reproach;   190
For I will leave my relics in your land,
And you may carve a shrine about my dust,
And burn a fragrant lamp before my bones,
When I am gather'd to the glorious saints.

While I spake then, a sting of shrewdest pain   195
Ran shrivelling thro' me, and a cloudlike change,
In passing, with a grosser film made thick
These heavy, horny eyes. The end! the end!
Surely the end! What's here? a shape, a shade,
A flash of light. Is that the angel there   200
That holds a crown? Come, blessed brother, come.
I know thy glittering face. I waited long;
My brows are ready. What! deny it now?
Nay, draw, draw, draw nigh. So I clutch it. Christ!
'Tis gone: 'tis here again; the crown! the crown!   205
So now 'tis fitted on and grows to me,
And from it melt the dews of Paradise,
Sweet! sweet! spikenard, and balm, and frankincense.
Ah! let me not be fool'd, sweet saints: I trust

That I am whole, and clean, and meet for Heaven. 210
  Speak, if there be a priest, a man of God,
Among you there, and let him presently
Approach, and lean a ladder on the shaft,
And climbing up into my airy home,
Deliver me the blessed sacrament; 215
For by the warning of the Holy Ghost,
I prophesy that I shall die to-night,
A quarter before twelve.
                    But thou, O Lord,
Aid all this foolish people; let them take
Example, pattern: lead them to thy light. 220

Ulysses

Poems (1842)

IT little profits that an idle king,
By this still hearth, among these barren crags,
Match'd with an aged wife, I mete and dole
Unequal laws unto a savage race,
That hoard, and sleep, and feed, and know not me. 5
I cannot rest from travel: I will drink
Life to the lees: all times I have enjoy'd
Greatly, have suffer'd greatly, both with those
That loved me, and alone; on shore, and when
Thro' scudding drifts the rainy Hyades 10
Vext the dim sea: I am become a name;
For always roaming with a hungry heart
Much have I seen and known; cities of men
And manners, climates, councils, governments,
Myself not least, but honour'd of them all; 15
And drunk delight of battle with my peers,

Far on the ringing plains of windy Troy.
I am a part of all that I have met;
Yet all experience is an arch wherethro'
Gleams that untravell'd world, whose margin fades   20
For ever and for ever when I move.
How dull it is to pause, to make an end,
To rust unburnish'd, not to shine in use!
As tho' to breathe were life. Life piled on life
Were all too little, and of one to me   25
Little remains: but every hour is saved
From that eternal silence, something more,
A bringer of new things; and vile it were
For some three suns to store and hoard myself,
And this gray spirit yearning in desire   30
To follow knowledge like a sinking star,
Beyond the utmost bound of human thought.

  This is my son, mine own Telemachus,
To whom I leave the sceptre and the isle—
Well-loved of me, discerning to fulfil   35
This labour, by slow prudence to make mild
A rugged people, and thro' soft degrees
Subdue them to the useful and the good.
Most blameless is he, centred in the sphere
Of common duties, decent not to fail   40
In offices of tenderness, and pay
Meet adoration to my household gods,
When I am gone. He works his work, I mine.

  There lies the port; the vessel puffs her sail:
There gloom the dark broad seas. My mariners,   45
Souls that have toil'd, and wrought, and thought with me—
That ever with a frolic welcome took
The thunder and the sunshine, and opposed
Free hearts, free foreheads—you and I are old;

Old age hath yet his honour and his toil;   50
Death closes all: but something ere the end,
Some work of noble note, may yet be done,
Not unbecoming men that strove with Gods.
The lights begin to twinkle from the rocks:
The long day wanes: the slow moon climbs: the deep   55
Moans round with many voices. Come, my friends,
'Tis not too late to seek a newer world.
Push off, and sitting well in order smite
The sounding furrows; for my purpose holds
To sail beyond the sunset, and the baths   60
Of all the western stars, until I die.
It may be that the gulfs will wash us down:
It may be we shall touch the Happy Isles,
And see the great Achilles, whom we knew.
Tho' much is taken, much abides; and tho'   65
We are not now that strength which in old days
Moved earth and heaven; that which we are, we are;
One equal temper of heroic hearts,
Made weak by time and fate, but strong in will
To strive, to seek, to find, and not to yield.   70

Tithonus

Published 1860 (*Cornhill Magazine*); largely written in 1830's

THE woods decay, the woods decay and fall,
The vapours weep their burthen to the ground,
Man comes and tills the field and lies beneath,
And after many a summer dies the swan.
Me only cruel immortality   5
Consumes: I wither slowly in thine arms,
Here at the quiet limit of the world,

A white-hair'd shadow roaming like a dream
The ever-silent spaces of the East,
Far-folded mists, and gleaming halls of morn.   10

   Alas! for this gray shadow, once a man—
So glorious in his beauty and thy choice,
Who madest him thy chosen, that he seem'd
To his great heart none other than a God!
I ask'd thee, 'Give me immortality.'   15
Then didst thou grant mine asking with a smile,
Like wealthy men who care not how they give.
But thy strong Hours indignant work'd their wills,
And beat me down and marr'd and wasted me,
And tho' they could not end me, left me maim'd   20
To dwell in presence of immortal youth,
Immortal age beside immortal youth,
And all I was, in ashes. Can thy love,
Thy beauty, make amends, tho' even now,
Close over us, the silver star, thy guide,   25
Shines in those tremulous eyes that fill with tears
To hear me? Let me go: take back thy gift:
Why should a man desire in any way
To vary from the kindly race of men,
Or pass beyond the goal of ordinance   30
Where all should pause, as is most meet for all?

   A soft air fans the cloud apart; there comes
A glimpse of that dark world where I was born.
Once more the old mysterious glimmer steals
From thy pure brows, and from thy shoulders pure,   35
And bosom beating with a heart renew'd.
Thy cheek begins to redden thro' the gloom,
Thy sweet eyes brighten slowly close to mine,

Ere yet they blind the stars, and the wild team
Which love thee, yearning for thy yoke, arise,   40
And shake the darkness from their loosen'd manes,
And beat the twilight into flakes of fire.

  Lo! ever thus thou growest beautiful
In silence, then before thine answer given
Departest, and thy tears are on my cheek.   45

  Why wilt thou ever scare me with thy tears,
And make me tremble lest a saying learnt,
In days far-off, on that dark earth, be true?
'The Gods themselves cannot recall their gifts.'

  Ay me! ay me! with what another heart   50
In days far-off, and with what other eyes
I used to watch—if I be he that watch'd—
The lucid outline forming round thee; saw
The dim curls kindle into sunny rings;
Changed with thy mystic change, and felt my blood   55
Glow with the glow that slowly crimson'd all
Thy presence and thy portals, while I lay,
Mouth, forehead, eyelids, growing dewy-warm
With kisses balmier than half-opening buds
Of April, and could hear the lips that kiss'd   60
Whispering I knew not what of wild and sweet,
Like that strange song I heard Apollo sing,
While Ilion like a mist rose into towers.

  Yet hold me not for ever in thine East:
How can my nature longer mix with thine?   65
Coldly thy rosy shadows bathe me, cold
Are all thy lights, and cold my wrinkled feet

Upon thy glimmering thresholds, when the steam
Floats up from those dim fields about the homes
Of happy men that have the power to die,   70
And grassy barrows of the happier dead.
Release me, and restore me to the ground;
Thou seëst all things, thou wilt see my grave:
Thou wilt renew thy beauty morn by morn;
I earth in earth forget these empty courts,   75
And thee returning on thy silver wheels.

Locksley Hall

Poems (1842)

COMRADES, leave me here a little, while as yet 'tis early morn:
Leave me here, and when you want me, sound upon the
    bugle-horn.

'Tis the place, and all around it, as of old, the curlews call,
Dreary gleams about the moorland flying over Locksley Hall;

Locksley Hall, that in the distance overlooks the sandy tracts, 5
And the hollow ocean-ridges roaring into cataracts.

Many a night from yonder ivied casement, ere I went to rest,
Did I look on great Orion sloping slowly to the West.

Many a night I saw the Pleiads, rising thro' the mellow shade,
Glitter like a swarm of fire-flies tangled in a silver braid.   10

Here about the beach I wander'd, nourishing a youth sublime
With the fairy tales of science, and the long result of Time;

When the centuries behind me like a fruitful land reposed;
When I clung to all the present for the promise that it closed:

When I dipt into the future far as human eye could see;　15
Saw the Vision of the world, and all the wonder that would
　　be.——

In the Spring a fuller crimson comes upon the robin's breast;
In the Spring the wanton lapwing gets himself another crest;

In the Spring a livelier iris changes on the burnish'd dove;
In the Spring a young man's fancy lightly turns to thoughts of
　　love.　20

Then her cheek was pale and thinner than should be for one so
　　young,
And her eyes on all my motions with a mute observance
　　hung.

And I said, 'My cousin Amy, speak, and speak the truth to
　　me,
Trust me, cousin, all the current of my being sets to thee.'

On her pallid cheek and forehead came a colour and a light,　25
As I have seen the rosy red flushing in the northern night.

And she turn'd—her bosom shaken with a sudden storm of
　　sighs—
All the spirit deeply dawning in the dark of hazel eyes—

Saying, 'I have hid my feelings, fearing they should do me
　　wrong;'
Saying, 'Dost thou love me, cousin?' weeping, 'I have loved
　　thee long.'　30

Love took up the glass of Time, and turn'd it in his glowing
　　hands;
Every moment, lightly shaken, ran itself in golden sands.

Love took up the harp of Life, and smote on all the chords
    with might;
Smote the chord of Self, that, trembling, pass'd in music out
    of sight.

Many a morning on the moorland did we hear the copses ring,
And her whisper throng'd my pulses with the fulness of the
    Spring.   36

Many an evening by the waters did we watch the stately ships,
And our spirits rush'd together at the touching of the lips.

O my cousin, shallow-hearted! O my Amy, mine no more!
O the dreary, dreary moorland! O the barren, barren shore! 40

Falser than all fancy fathoms, falser than all songs have sung,
Puppet to a father's threat, and servile to a shrewish tongue!

Is it well to wish thee happy?—having known me—to decline
On a range of lower feelings and a narrower heart than mine!

Yet it shall be: thou shalt lower to his level day by day,   45
What is fine within thee growing coarse to sympathise with
    clay.

As the husband is, the wife is: thou art mated with a clown,
And the grossness of his nature will have weight to drag thee
    down.

He will hold thee, when his passion shall have spent its novel
    force,
Something better than his dog, a little dearer than his horse. 50

What is this? his eyes are heavy: think not they are glazed
    with wine.
Go to him: it is thy duty: kiss him: take his hand in thine.

It may be my lord is weary, that his brain is overwrought:
Soothe him with thy finer fancies, touch him with thy lighter
    thought.

He will answer to the purpose, easy things to understand— 55
Better thou wert dead before me, tho' I slew thee with my
    hand!

Better thou and I were lying, hidden from the heart's disgrace,
Roll'd in one another's arms, and silent in a last embrace.

Cursed be the social wants that sin against the strength of
    youth!
Cursed be the social lies that warp us from the living truth! 60

Cursed be the sickly forms that err from honest Nature's rule!
Cursed be the gold that gilds the straiten'd forehead of the
    fool!

Well—'tis well that I should bluster!—Hadst thou less un-
    worthy proved—
Would to God—for I had loved thee more than ever wife was
    loved.

Am I mad, that I should cherish that which bears but bitter
    fruit?   65
I will pluck it from my bosom, tho' my heart be at the root.

Never, tho' my mortal summers to such length of years
    should come
As the many-winter'd crow that leads the clanging rookery
    home.

Where is comfort? in division of the records of the mind?
Can I part her from herself, and love her, as I knew her,
    kind?   70

I remember one that perish'd: sweetly did she speak and move:
Such a one do I remember, whom to look at was to love.

Can I think of her as dead, and love her for the love she bore?
No—she never loved me truly: love is love for evermore.

Comfort? comfort scorn'd of devils! this is truth the poet
    sings,   75
That a sorrow's crown of sorrow is remembering happier
    things.

Drug thy memories, lest thou learn it, lest thy heart be put to
    proof,
In the dead unhappy night, and when the rain is on the roof.

Like a dog, he hunts in dreams, and thou art staring at the wall,
Where the dying night-lamp flickers, and the shadows rise and
    fall.   80

Then a hand shall pass before thee, pointing to his drunken
    sleep,
To thy widow'd marriage-pillows, to the tears that thou wilt
    weep.

Thou shalt hear the 'Never, never,' whisper'd by the phantom
    years,
And a song from out the distance in the ringing of thine ears;

And an eye shall vex thee, looking ancient kindness on thy
    pain.   85
Turn thee, turn thee on thy pillow: get thee to thy rest again.

Nay, but Nature brings thee solace; for a tender voice will cry.
'Tis a purer life than thine; a lip to drain thy trouble dry.

Baby lips will laugh me down: my latest rival brings thee rest.
Baby fingers, waxen touches, press me from the mother's
  breast.   90

O, the child too clothes the father with a dearness not his
  due.
Half is thine and half is his: it will be worthy of the two.

O, I see thee old and formal, fitted to thy petty part,
With a little hoard of maxims preaching down a daughter's
  heart.

'They were dangerous guides the feelings—she herself was not
  exempt—   95
Truly, she herself had suffer'd'—Perish in thy self-contempt!

Overlive it—lower yet—be happy! wherefore should I care?
I myself must mix with action, lest I wither by despair.

What is that which I should turn to, lighting upon days like
  these?
Every door is barr'd with gold, and opens but to golden
  keys.   100

Every gate is throng'd with suitors, all the markets overflow.
I have but an angry fancy: what is that which I should do?

I had been content to perish, falling on the foeman's ground,
When the ranks are roll'd in vapour, and the winds are laid
  with sound.

But the jingling of the guinea helps the hurt that Honour
  feels,   105
And the nations do but murmur, snarling at each other's
  heels.

Can I but relive in sadness? I will turn that earlier page.
Hide me from my deep emotion, O thou wondrous Mother-
    Age!

Make me feel the wild pulsation that I felt before the strife,
When I heard my days before me, and the tumult of my
    life;   110

Yearning for the large excitement that the coming years
    would yield,
Eager-hearted as a boy when first he leaves his father's field,

And at night along the dusky highway near and nearer drawn,
Sees in heaven the light of London flaring like a dreary dawn;

And his spirit leaps within him to be gone before him then, 115
Underneath the light he looks at, in among the throngs of
    men:

Men, my brothers, men the workers, ever reaping something
    new:
That which they have done but earnest of the things that they
    shall do:

For I dipt into the future, far as human eye could see,
Saw the Vision of the world, and all the wonder that would
    be;   120

Saw the heavens fill with commerce, argosies of magic sails,
Pilots of the purple twilight, dropping down with costly
    bales;

Heard the heavens fill with shouting, and there rain'd a ghastly
    dew
From the nations' airy navies grappling in the central blue;

Far along the world-wide whisper of the south-wind rushing
    warm,   125
With the standards of the peoples plunging thro' the thunder-
    storm;

Till the war-drum throbb'd no longer, and the battle-flags
    were furl'd
In the Parliament of man, the Federation of the world.

There the common sense of most shall hold a fretful realm in
    awe,
And the kindly earth shall slumber, lapt in universal law.   130

So I triumph'd ere my passion sweeping thro' me left me
    dry,
Left me with the palsied heart, and left me with the jaun-
    diced eye;

Eye, to which all order festers, all things here are out of joint:
Science moves, but slowly slowly, creeping on from point to
    point:

Slowly comes a hungry people, as a lion creeping nigher,   135
Glares at one that nods and winks behind a slowly-dying fire.

Yet I doubt not thro' the ages one increasing purpose runs,
And the thoughts of men are widen'd with the process of the
    suns.

What is that to him that reaps not harvest of his youthful joys,
Tho' the deep heart of existence beat for ever like a boy's?   140

Knowledge comes, but wisdom lingers, and I linger on the
    shore,
And the individual withers, and the world is more and more.

Knowledge comes, but wisdom lingers, and he bears a laden
    breast,
Full of sad experience, moving toward the stillness of his rest.

Hark, my merry comrades call me, sounding on the bugle-
    horn,   145
They to whom my foolish passion were a target for their
    scorn:

Shall it not be scorn to me to harp on such a moulder'd string?
I am shamed thro' all my nature to have loved so slight a
    thing.

Weakness to be wroth with weakness! woman's pleasure,
    woman's pain—
Nature made them blinder motions bounded in a shallower
    brain: 150

Woman is the lesser man, and all thy passions, match'd with
    mine,
Are as moonlight unto sunlight, and as water unto wine—

Here at least, where nature sickens, nothing. Ah, for some
    retreat
Deep in yonder shining Orient, where my life began to beat;

Where in wild Mahratta-battle fell my father evil-starr'd;—155
I was left a trampled orphan, and a selfish uncle's ward.

Or to burst all links of habit—there to wander far away,
On from island unto island at the gateways of the day.

Larger constellations burning, mellow moons and happy skies,
Breadths of tropic shade and palms in cluster, knots of Para-
    dise.   160

Never comes the trader, never floats an European flag,
Slides the bird o'er lustrous woodland, swings the trailer from
    the crag;

Droops the heavy-blossom'd bower, hangs the heavy-fruited
    tree—
Summer isles of Eden lying in dark-purple spheres of sea.

There methinks would be enjoyment more than in this march
    of mind,   165
In the steamship, in the railway, in the thoughts that shake
    mankind.

There the passions cramp'd no longer shall have scope and
    breathing space;
I will take some savage woman, she shall rear my dusky race.

Iron jointed, supple-sinew'd, they shall dive, and they shall
    run,
Catch the wild goat by the hair, and hurl their lances in the
    sun;   170

Whistle back the parrot's call, and leap the rainbows of the
    brooks,
Not with blinded eyesight poring over miserable books—

Fool, again the dream, the fancy! but I *know* my words are
    wild,
But I count the gray barbarian lower than the Christian child.

I, to herd with narrow foreheads, vacant of our glorious
    gains,   175
Like a beast with lower pleasures, like a beast with lower pains!

Mated with a squalid savage—what to me were sun or clime?
I the heir of all the ages, in the foremost files of time—

I that rather held it better men should perish one by one,
Than that earth should stand at gaze like Joshua's moon in
    Ajalon! 180

Not in vain the distance beacons. Forward, forward let us range,
Let the great world spin for ever down the ringing grooves of
    change.

Thro' the shadow of the globe we sweep into the younger
    day:
Better fifty years of Europe than a cycle of Cathay.

Mother-Age (for mine I knew not) help me as when life
    begun: 185
Rift the hills, and roll the waters, flash the lightnings, weigh the
    Sun.

O, I see the crescent promise of my spirit hath not set.
Ancient founts of inspiration well thro' all my fancy yet.

Howsoever these things be, a long farewell to Locksley Hall!
Now for me the woods may wither, now for me the roof-tree
    fall. 190

Comes a vapour from the margin, blackening over heath and
    holt,
Cramming all the blast before it, in its breast a thunderbolt.

Let it fall on Locksley Hall, with rain or hail, or fire or snow;
For the mighty wind arises, roaring seaward, and I go.

The Two Voices

Poems (1842)

A STILL small voice spake unto me,
'Thou art so full of misery,
Were it not better not to be?'

Then to the still small voice I said;
'Let me not cast in endless shade   5
What is so wonderfully made.'

To which the voice did urge reply;
'To-day I saw the dragon-fly
Come from the wells where he did lie.

'An inner impulse rent the veil   10
Of his old husk: from head to tail
Came out clear plates of sapphire mail.

'He dried his wings: like gauze they grew;
Thro' crofts and pastures wet with dew
A living flash of light he flew.'   15

I said, 'When first the world began,
Young Nature thro' five cycles ran,
And in the sixth she moulded man.

'She gave him mind, the lordliest
Proportion, and, above the rest,   20
Dominion in the head and breast.'

Thereto the silent voice replied;
'Self-blinded are you by your pride:
Look up thro' night: the world is wide.

'This truth within thy mind rehearse,   25
That in a boundless universe
Is boundless better, boundless worse.

'Think you this mould of hopes and fears
Could find no statelier than his peers
In yonder hundred million spheres?'   30

It spake, moreover, in my mind:
'Tho' thou wert scatter'd to the wind,
Yet is there plenty of the kind.'

Then did my response clearer fall:
'No compound of this earthly ball   35
Is like another, all in all.'

To which he answer'd scoffingly;
'Good soul! suppose I grant it thee,
Who'll weep for thy deficiency?

'Or will one beam be less intense,   40
When thy peculiar difference
Is cancell'd in the world of sense?'

I would have said, 'Thou canst not know,'
But my full heart, that work'd below,
Rain'd thro' my sight its overflow.   45

Again the voice spake unto me:
'Thou art so steep'd in misery,
Surely 'twere better not to be.

'Thine anguish will not let thee sleep,
Nor any train of reason keep: 50
Thou canst not think, but thou wilt weep.'

I said, 'The years with change advance:
If I make dark my countenance,
I shut my life from happier chance.

'Some turn this sickness yet might take,   55
Ev'n yet.' But he: 'What drug can make
A wither'd palsy cease to shake?'

I wept, 'Tho' I should die, I know
That all about the thorn will blow
In tufts of rosy-tinted snow;   60

'And men, thro' novel spheres of thought
Still moving after truth long sought,
Will learn new things when I am not.'

'Yet,' said the secret voice, 'some time,
Sooner or later, will gray prime   65
Make thy grass hoar with early rime.

'Not less swift souls that yearn for light,
Rapt after heaven's starry flight,
Would sweep the tracts of day and night.

'Not less the bee would range her cells,   70
The furzy prickle fire the dells,
The foxglove cluster dappled bells.'

I said that 'all the years invent;
Each month is various to present
The world with some development.   75

'Were this not well, to bide mine hour,
Tho' watching from a ruin'd tower
How grows the day of human power?'

'The highest-mounted mind,' he said,
'Still sees the sacred morning spread   80
The silent summit overhead.

'Will thirty seasons render plain
Those lonely lights that still remain,
Just breaking over land and main?

'Or make that morn, from his cold crown   85
And crystal silence creeping down,
Flood with full daylight glebe and town?

'Forerun thy peers, thy time, and let
Thy feet, millenniums hence, be set
In midst of knowledge, dream'd not yet.   90

'Thou hast not gain'd a real height,
Nor art thou nearer to the light,
Because the scale is infinite.

''Twere better not to breathe or speak,
Than cry for strength, remaining weak,   95
And seem to find, but still to seek.

'Moreover, but to seem to find
Asks what thou lackest, thought resign'd,
A healthy frame, a quiet mind.'

I said, 'When I am gone away,   100
"He dared not tarry," men will say,
Doing dishonour to my clay.'

'This is more vile,' he made reply,
'To breathe and loathe, to live and sigh,
Than once from dread of pain to die.   105

'Sick art thou—a divided will
Still heaping on the fear of ill
The fear of men, a coward still.

'Do men love thee? Art thou so bound
To men, that how thy name may sound   110
Will vex thee lying underground?

'The memory of the wither'd leaf
In endless time is scarce more brief
Than of the garner'd Autumn-sheaf.

'Go, vexed Spirit, sleep in trust;   115
The right ear, that is fill'd with dust,
Hears little of the false or just.'

'Hard task, to pluck resolve,' I cried,
'From emptiness and the waste wide
Of that abyss, or scornful pride!   120

'Nay—rather yet that I could raise
One hope that warm'd me in the days
While still I yearn'd for human praise.

'When, wide in soul and bold of tongue,
Among the tents I paused and sung,   125
The distant battle flash'd and rung.

'I sung the joyful Pæan clear,
And, sitting, burnish'd without fear
The brand, the buckler, and the spear—

'Waiting to strive a happy strife,   130
To war with falsehood to the knife,
And not to lose the good of life—

'Some hidden principle to move,
To put together, part and prove,
And mete the bounds of hate and love—   135

'As far as might be, to carve out
Free space for every human doubt,
That the whole mind might orb about—

'To search thro' all I felt or saw,
The springs of life, the depths of awe,   140
And reach the law within the law:

'At least, not rotting like a weed,
But, having sown some generous seed,
Fruitful of further thought and deed,

'To pass, when Life her light withdraws,   145
Not void of righteous self-applause,
Nor in a merely selfish cause—

'In some good cause, not in mine own,
To perish, wept for, honour'd, known,
And like a warrior overthrown;   150

'Whose eyes are dim with glorious tears,
When, soil'd with noble dust, he hears
His country's war-song thrill his ears:

'Then dying of a mortal stroke,
What time the foeman's line is broke,   155
And all the war is roll'd in smoke.'

'Yea!' said the voice, 'thy dream was good,
While thou abodest in the bud.
It was the stirring of the blood.

'If Nature put not forth her power   160
About the opening of the flower,
Who is it that could live an hour?

'Then comes the check, the change, the fall,
Pain rises up, old pleasures pall.
There is one remedy for all.   165

'Yet hadst thou, thro' enduring pain,
Link'd month to month with such a chain
Of knitted purport, all were vain.

'Thou hadst not between death and birth
Dissolved the riddle of the earth.   170
So were thy labour little-worth.

'That men with knowledge merely play'd,
I told thee—hardly nigher made,
Tho' scaling slow from grade to grade;

'Much less this dreamer, deaf and blind,   175
Named man, may hope some truth to find,
That bears relation to the mind.

'For every worm beneath the moon
Draws different threads, and late and soon
Spins, toiling out his own cocoon.   180

'Cry, faint not: either Truth is born
Beyond the polar gleam forlorn,
Or in the gateways of the morn.

'Cry, faint not, climb: the summits slope
Beyond the furthest flights of hope,   185
Wrapt in dense cloud from base to cope.

'Sometimes a little corner shines,
As over rainy mist inclines
A gleaming crag with belts of pines.

'I will go forward, sayest thou,   190
I shall not fail to find her now.
Look up, the fold is on her brow.

'If straight thy track, or if oblique,
Thou know'st not. Shadows thou dost strike,
Embracing cloud, Ixion-like;   195

'And owning but a little more
Than beasts, abidest lame and poor,
Calling thyself a little lower

'Than angels. Cease to wail and brawl!
Why inch by inch to darkness crawl?   200
There is one remedy for all.'

'O dull, one-sided voice,' said I,
'Wilt thou make everything a lie,
To flatter me that I may die?

'I know that age to age succeeds,   205
Blowing a noise of tongues and deeds,
A dust of systems and of creeds.

'I cannot hide that some have striven,
Achieving calm, to whom was given
The joy that mixes man with Heaven: 210

'Who, rowing hard against the stream,
Saw distant gates of Eden gleam,
And did not dream it was a dream;

'But heard, by secret transport led,
Ev'n in the charnels of the dead,   215
The murmur of the fountain-head—

'Which did accomplish their desire,
Bore and forbore, and did not tire,
Like Stephen, an unquenched fire.

'He heeded not reviling tones,   220
Nor sold his heart to idle moans,
Tho' cursed and scorn'd, and bruised with stones:

'But looking upward, full of grace,
He pray'd, and from a happy place
God's glory smote him on the face.'   225

The sullen answer slid betwixt:
'Not that the grounds of hope were fix'd,
The elements were kindlier mix'd.'

I said, 'I toil beneath the curse,
But, knowing not the universe,   230
I fear to slide from bad to worse.

'And that, in seeking to undo
One riddle, and to find the true,
I knit a hundred others new:

'Or that this anguish fleeting hence,   235
Unmanacled from bonds of sense,
Be fix'd and froz'n to permanence:

'For I go, weak from suffering here:
Naked I go, and void of cheer:
What is it that I may not fear?'   240

'Consider well,' the voice replied,
'His face, that two hours since hath died;
Wilt thou find passion, pain or pride?

'Will he obey when one commands?   245
Or answer should one press his hands?
He answers not, nor understands.

'His palms are folded on his breast:
There is no other thing express'd
But long disquiet merged in rest.

'His lips are very mild and meek: 250
Tho' one should smite him on the cheek,
And on the mouth, he will not speak.

'His little daughter, whose sweet face
He kiss'd, taking his last embrace,
Becomes dishonour to her race—   255

'His sons grow up that bear his name,
Some grow to honour, some to shame,—
But he is chill to praise or blame.

'He will not hear the north-wind rave,
Nor, moaning, household shelter crave   260
From winter rains that beat his grave.

'High up the vapours fold and swim:
About him broods the twilight dim:
The place he knew forgetteth him.'

'If all be dark, vague voice,' I said,   265
'These things are wrapt in doubt and dread,
Nor canst thou show the dead are dead.

'The sap dries up: the plant declines.
A deeper tale my heart divines.
Know I not Death? the outward signs?   270

'I found him when my years were few;
A shadow on the graves I knew,
And darkness in the village yew.

'From grave to grave the shadow crept:
In her still place the morning wept: 275
Touch'd by his feet the daisy slept.

'The simple senses crown'd his head:
"Omega! thou art Lord," they said,
"We find no motion in the dead."

'Why, if man rot in dreamless ease,   280
Should that plain fact, as taught by these,
Not make him sure that he shall cease?

'Who forged that other influence,
That heat of inward evidence,
By which he doubts against the sense?   285

'He owns the fatal gift of eyes,
That read his spirit blindly wise,
Not simple as a thing that dies.

'Here sits he shaping wings to fly:
His heart forebodes a mystery: 290
He names the name Eternity.

'That type of Perfect in his mind
In Nature can he nowhere find.
He sows himself on every wind.

'He seems to hear a Heavenly Friend,   295
And thro' thick veils to apprehend
A labour working to an end.

'The end and the beginning vex
His reason: many things perplex,
With motions, checks, and counterchecks.   300

'He knows a baseness in his blood
At such strange war with something good,
He may not do the thing he would.

'Heaven opens inward, chasms yawn,
Vast images in glimmering dawn,   305
Half shown, are broken and withdrawn.

'Ah! sure within him and without,
Could his dark wisdom find it out,
There must be answer to his doubt.

'But thou canst answer not again.   310
With thine own weapon art thou slain,
Or thou wilt answer but in vain.

'The doubt would rest, I dare not solve.
In the same circle we revolve.
Assurance only breeds resolve.'   315

As when a billow, blown against,
Falls back, the voice with which I fenced
A little ceased, but recommenced.

'Where wert thou when thy father play'd
In his free field, and pastime made,   320
A merry boy in sun and shade?

'A merry boy they call'd him then,
He sat upon the knees of men
In days that never come again.

'Before the little ducts began   325
To feed thy bones with lime, and ran
Their course, till thou wert also man:

'Who took a wife, who rear'd his race,
Whose wrinkles gather'd on his face,
Whose troubles number with his days: 330

'A life of nothings, nothing-worth,
From that first nothing ere his birth
To that last nothing under earth!'

'These words,' I said, 'are like the rest;
No certain clearness, but at best   335
A vague suspicion of the breast:

'But if I grant, thou mightst defend
The thesis which thy words intend—
That to begin implies to end;

'Yet how should I for certain hold,   340
Because my memory is so cold,
That I first was in human mould?

'I cannot make this matter plain,
But I would shoot, howe'er in vain,
A random arrow from the brain.   345

'It may be that no life is found,
Which only to one engine bound
Falls off, but cycles always round.

'As old mythologies relate,
Some draught of Lethe might await   350
The slipping thro' from state to state.

'As here we find in trances, men
Forget the dream that happens then,
Until they fall in trance again.

'So might we, if our state were such   355
As one before, remember much,
For those two likes might meet and touch.

'But, if I lapsed from nobler place,
Some legend of a fallen race
Alone might hint of my disgrace;   360

'Some vague emotion of delight
In gazing up an Alpine height,
Some yearning toward the lamps of night;

'Or if thro' lower lives I came—
Tho' all experience past became   365
Consolidate in mind and frame—

'I might forget my weaker lot;
For is not our first year forgot?
The haunts of memory echo not.

'And men, whose reason long was blind,   370
From cells of madness unconfined,
Oft lose whole years of darker mind.

'Much more, if first I floated free,
As naked essence, must I be
Incompetent of memory: 375

'For memory dealing but with time,
And he with matter, could she climb
Beyond her own material prime?

'Moreover, something is or seems,
That touches me with mystic gleams,   380
Like glimpses of forgotten dreams—

'Of something felt, like something here;
Of something done, I know not where;
Such as no language may declare.'

The still voice laugh'd. 'I talk,' said he,   385
'Not with thy dreams. Suffice it thee
Thy pain is a reality.'

'But thou,' said I, 'hast missed thy mark,
Who sought'st to wreck my mortal ark,
By making all the horizon dark.   390

'Why not set forth, if I should do
This rashness, that which might ensue
With this old soul in organs new?

'Whatever crazy sorrow saith,
No life that breathes with human breath   395
Has ever truly long'd for death.

''Tis life, whereof our nerves are scant,
Oh life, not death, for which we pant;
More life, and fuller, that I want.'

I ceased, and sat as one forlorn.   400
Then said the voice, in quiet scorn,
'Behold, it is the Sabbath morn.'

And I arose, and I released
The casement, and the light increased
With freshness in the dawning east.   405

Like soften'd airs that blowing steal,
When meres begin to uncongeal,
The sweet church bells began to peal.

On to God's house the people prest:
Passing the place where each must rest,   410
Each enter'd like a welcome guest.

One walk'd between his wife and child,
With measured footfall firm and mild,
And now and then he gravely smiled.

The prudent partner of his blood   415
Lean'd on him, faithful, gentle, good,
Wearing the rose of womanhood.

And in their double love secure,
The little maiden walk'd demure,
Pacing with downward eyelids pure.   420

These three made unity so sweet,
My frozen heart began to beat,
Remembering its ancient heat.

I blest them, and they wander'd on:
I spoke, but answer came there none: 425
The dull and bitter voice was gone.

A second voice was at mine ear,
A little whisper silver-clear,
A murmur, 'Be of better cheer.'

As from some blissful neighbourhood,   430
A notice faintly understood,
'I see the end, and know the good.'

A little hint to solace woe,
A hint, a whisper breathing low,
'I may not speak of what I know.'   435

Like an Æolian harp that wakes
No certain air, but overtakes
Far thought with music that it makes:

Such seem'd the whisper at my side:
'What is it thou knowest, sweet voice?' I cried.   440
'A hidden hope,' the voice replied:

So heavenly-toned, that in that hour
From out my sullen heart a power
Broke, like the rainbow from the shower,

To feel, altho' no tongue can prove,   445
That every cloud, that spreads above
And veileth love, itself is love.

And forth into the fields I went,
And Nature's living motion lent
The pulse of hope to discontent.   450

I wonder'd at the bounteous hours,
The slow result of winter showers:
You scarce could see the grass for flowers.

I wonder'd, while I paced along:
The woods were fill'd so full with song,   455
There seem'd no room for sense of wrong;

And all so variously wrought,
I marvell'd how the mind was brought
To anchor by one gloomy thought;

And wherefore rather I made choice   460
To commune with that barren voice,
Than him that said, 'Rejoice! Rejoice!'

From Will Waterproof's Lyrical Monologue

Poems (1842)

MADE AT THE COCK

O PLUMP head-waiter at The Cock,
   To which I most resort,
How goes the time? 'Tis five o'clock.
   Go fetch a pint of port:
But let it not be such as that   5
   You set before chance-comers,
But such whose father-grape grew fat
   On Lusitanian summers.

No vain libation to the Muse,
   But may she still be kind,   10
And whisper lovely words, and use
   Her influence on the mind,
To make me write my random rhymes,
   Ere they be half-forgotten;
Nor add and alter, many times,   15
   Till all be ripe and rotten.

I pledge her, and she comes and dips
    Her laurel in the wine,
And lays it thrice upon my lips,
    These favour'd lips of mine;   20
Until the charm have power to make
    New lifeblood warm the bosom,
And barren commonplaces break
    In full and kindly blossom.

I pledge her silent at the board;   25
    Her gradual fingers steal
And touch upon the master-chord
    Of all I felt and feel.
Old wishes, ghosts of broken plans,
    And phantom hopes assemble;   30
And that child's heart within the man's
    Begins to move and tremble.

Thro' many an hour of summer suns,
    By many pleasant ways,
Against its fountain upward runs   35
    The current of my days:
I kiss the lips I once have kiss'd;
    The gas-light wavers dimmer;
And softly, thro' a vinous mist,
    My college friendships glimmer.   40

I grow in worth, and wit, and sense,
    Unboding critic-pen,
Or that eternal want of pence,
    Which vexes public men,
Who hold their hands to all, and cry   45
    For that which all deny them—
Who sweep the crossings, wet or dry,
    And all the world go by them.

Ah yet, tho' all the world forsake,
   Tho' fortune clip my wings,   50
I will not cramp my heart, nor take
   Half-views of men and things.
Let Whig and Tory stir their blood;
   There must be stormy weather;
But for some true result of good   55
   All parties work together.

Let there be thistles, there are grapes;
   If old things, there are new;
Ten thousand broken lights and shapes,
   Yet glimpses of the true.   60
Let raffs be rife in prose and rhyme,
   We lack not rhymes and reasons,
As on this whirligig of Time
   We circle with the seasons.

This earth is rich in man and maid;   65
   With fair horizons bound:
This whole wide earth of light and shade
   Comes out a perfect round.
High over roaring Temple-bar,
   And set in Heaven's third story,   70
I look at all things as they are,
   But thro' a kind of glory.

. . . .

The Vision of Sin

Poems (1842)

I

I HAD a vision when the night was late:
A youth came riding toward a palace-gate.
He rode a horse with wings, that would have flown,
But that his heavy rider kept him down.
And from the palace came a child of sin,   5
And took him by the curls, and led him in,
Where sat a company with heated eyes,
Expecting when a fountain should arise:
A sleepy light upon their brows and lips—
As when the sun, a crescent of eclipse,   10
Dreams over lake and lawn, and isles and capes—
Suffused them, sitting, lying, languid shapes,
By heaps of gourds, and skins of wine, and piles of
      grapes.

II

Then methought I heard a mellow sound,
Gathering up from all the lower ground;   15
Narrowing in to where they sat assembled
Low voluptuous music winding trembled,
Wov'n in circles: they that heard it sigh'd,
Panted hand-in-hand with faces pale,
Swung themselves, and in low tones replied;   20
Till the fountain spouted, showering wide
Sleet of diamond-drift and pearly hail;
Then the music touch'd the gates and died;
Rose again from where it seem'd to fail,
Storm'd in orbs of song, a growing gale;   25

Till thronging in and in, to where they waited,
As 'twere a hundred-throated nightingale,
The strong tempestuous treble throbb'd and palpitated;
Ran into its giddiest whirl of sound,
Caught the sparkles, and in circles,   30
Purple gauzes, golden hazes, liquid mazes,
Flung the torrent rainbow round:
Then they started from their places,
Moved with violence, changed in hue,
Caught each other with wild grimaces,   35
Half-invisible to the view,
Wheeling with precipitate paces
To the melody, till they flew,
Hair, and eyes, and limbs, and faces,
Twisted hard in fierce embraces,   40
Like to Furies, like to Graces,
Dash'd together in blinding dew:
Till, kill'd with some luxurious agony,
The nerve-dissolving melody
Flutter'd headlong from the sky.   45

III

And then I look'd up toward a mountain-tract,
That girt the region with high cliff and lawn:
I saw that every morning, far withdrawn
Beyond the darkness and the cataract,
God made Himself an awful rose of dawn,   50
Unheeded: and detaching, fold by fold,
From those still heights, and, slowly drawing near,
A vapour heavy, hueless, formless, cold,
Came floating on for many a month and year,
Unheeded: and I thought I would have spoken,   55
And warn'd that madman ere it grew too late:

But, as in dreams, I could not. Mine was broken,
When that cold vapour touch'd the palace gate,
And link'd again. I saw within my head
A gray and gap-tooth'd man as lean as death,   60
Who slowly rode across a wither'd heath,
And lighted at a ruin'd inn, and said:

IV

'Wrinkled ostler, grim and thin!
    Here is custom come your way;
Take my brute, and lead him in,   65
    Stuff his ribs with mouldy hay.

'Bitter barmaid, waning fast!
    See that sheets are on my bed;
What! the flower of life is past:
    It is long before you wed.   70

'Slip-shod waiter, lank and sour,
    At the Dragon on the heath!
Let us have a quiet hour,
    Let us hob-and-nob with Death.

'I am old, but let me drink;   75
    Bring me spices, bring me wine;
I remember, when I think,
    That my youth was half divine.

'Wine is good for shrivell'd lips,
    When a blanket wraps the day,   80
When the rotten woodland drips,
    And the leaf is stamp'd in clay.

'Sit thee down, and have no shame,
  Cheek by jowl, and knee by knee:
What care I for any name?   85
  What for order or degree?

'Let me screw thee up a peg:
  Let me loose thy tongue with wine:
Callest thou that thing a leg?
  Which is thinnest? thine or mine?   90

'Thou shalt not be saved by works:
  Thou hast been a sinner too:
Ruin'd trunks on wither'd forks,
  Empty scarecrows, I and you!

'Fill the cup, and fill the can: 95
  Have a rouse before the morn:
Every moment dies a man,
  Every moment one is born.

'We are men of ruin'd blood;
  Therefore comes it we are wise.   100
Fish are we that love the mud,
  Rising to no fancy-flies.

'Name and fame! to fly sublime
  Thro' the courts, the camps, the schools,
Is to be the ball of Time,   105
  Bandied by the hands of fools.

'Friendship!—to be two in one—
  Let the canting liar pack!
Well I know, when I am gone,
  How she mouths behind my back.   110

'Virtue!—to be good and just—
　　Every heart, when sifted well,
Is a clot of warmer dust,
　　Mix'd with cunning sparks of hell.

'O! we two as well can look   115
　　Whited thought and cleanly life
As the priest, above his book
　　Leering at his neighbour's wife.

'Fill the cup, and fill the can:
　　Have a rouse before the morn: 120
Every moment dies a man,
　　Every moment one is born.

'Drink, and let the parties rave:
　　They are fill'd with idle spleen;
Rising, falling, like a wave,   125
　　For they know not what they mean.

'He that roars for liberty
　　Faster binds a tyrant's power;
And the tyrant's cruel glee
　　Forces on the freer hour.   130

'Fill the can, and fill the cup:
　　All the windy ways of men
Are but dust that rises up,
　　And is lightly laid again.

'Greet her with applausive breath,   135
　　Freedom, gaily doth she tread;
In her right a civic wreath,
　　In her left a human head.

'No, I love not what is new;
 She is of an ancient house: 140
And I think we know the hue
 Of that cap upon her brows.

'Let her go! her thirst she slakes
 Where the bloody conduit runs,
Then her sweetest meal she makes 145
 On the first-born of her sons.

'Drink to lofty hopes that cool—
 Visions of a perfect State:
Drink we, last, the public fool,
 Frantic love and frantic hate.   150

'Chant me now some wicked stave,
 Till thy drooping courage rise,
And the glow-worm of the grave
 Glimmer in thy rheumy eyes.

'Fear not thou to loose thy tongue; 155
 Set thy hoary fancies free;
What is loathsome to the young
 Savours well to thee and me.

'Change, reverting to the years,
 When thy nerves could understand 160
What there is in loving tears,
 And the warmth of hand in hand.

'Tell me tales of thy first love—
 April hopes, the fools of chance;
Till the graves begin to move,   165
 And the dead begin to dance.

'Fill the can, and fill the cup:
　　All the windy ways of men
Are but dust that rises up,
　　And is lightly laid again.   170

'Trooping from their mouldy dens
　　The chap-fallen circle spreads:
Welcome, fellow-citizens,
　　Hollow hearts and empty heads!

'You are bones, and what of that?   175
　　Every face, however full,
Padded round with flesh and fat,
　　Is but modell'd on a skull.

'Death is king, and Vivat Rex!
　　Tread a measure on the stones,   180
Madam—if I know your sex,
　　From the fashion of your bones.

'No, I cannot praise the fire
　　In your eye—nor yet your lip:
All the more do I admire   185
　　Joints of cunning workmanship.

'Lo! God's likeness—the ground-plan—
　　Neither modell'd, glazed, nor framed:
Buss me, thou rough sketch of man,
　　Far too naked to be shamed!   190

'Drink to Fortune, drink to Chance,
　　While we keep a little breath!
Drink to heavy Ignorance!
　　Hob-and-nob with brother Death!

'Thou art mazed, the night is long,   195
  And the longer night is near:
What! I am not all as wrong
  As a bitter jest is dear.

'Youthful hopes, by scores, to all,
  When the locks are crisp and curl'd;   200
Unto me my maudlin gall
  And my mockeries of the world.

'Fill the cup, and fill the can:
  Mingle madness, mingle scorn!
Dregs of life, and lees of man: 205
  Yet we will not die forlorn.'

V

The voice grew faint: there came a further change:
Once more uprose the mystic mountain-range:
Below were men and horses pierced with worms,
And slowly quickening into lower forms;   210
By shards and scurf of salt, and scum of dross,
Old plash of rains, and refuse patch'd with moss.
Then some one spake: 'Behold! it was a crime
Of sense avenged by sense that wore with time.'
Another said: 'The crime of sense became   215
The crime of malice, and is equal blame.'
And one: 'He had not wholly quench'd his power;
A little grain of conscience made him sour.'
At last I heard a voice upon the slope
Cry to the summit, 'Is there any hope?'   220
To which an answer peal'd from that high land,
But in a tongue no man could understand;
And on the glimmering limit far withdrawn
God made Himself an awful rose of dawn.

'Break, Break, Break'

Poems (1842)

BREAK, break, break,
  On thy cold gray stones, O Sea!
And I would that my tongue could utter
  The thoughts that arise in me.

O well for the fisherman's boy,   5
  That he shouts with his sister at play!
O well for the sailor lad,
  That he sings in his boat on the bay!

And the stately ships go on
  To their haven under the hill;   10
But O for the touch of a vanish'd hand,
  And the sound of a voice that is still!

Break, break, break,
  At the foot of thy crags, O Sea!
But the tender grace of a day that is dead   15
  Will never come back to me.

From The Princess

Published 1847

'TEARS, IDLE TEARS'

'TEARS, idle tears, I know not what they mean,
Tears from the depth of some divine despair
Rise in the heart, and gather to the eyes,
In looking on the happy Autumn-fields,
And thinking of the days that are no more.   5

'Fresh as the first beam glittering on a sail,
That brings our friends up from the underworld,
Sad as the last which reddens over one
That sinks with all we love below the verge;
So sad, so fresh, the days that are no more.   10

'Ah, sad and strange as in dark summer dawns
The earliest pipe of half-awaken'd birds
To dying ears, when unto dying eyes
The casement slowly grows a glimmering square;
So sad, so strange, the days that are no more.   15

'Dear as remember'd kisses after death,
And sweet as those by hopeless fancy feign'd
On lips that are for others; deep as love,
Deep as first love, and wild with all regret;
O Death in Life, the days that are no more.'   20

'O SWALLOW, SWALLOW'

'O Swallow, Swallow, flying, flying South,
Fly to her, and fall upon her gilded eaves,
And tell her, tell her, what I tell to thee.

'O tell her, Swallow, thou that knowest each,
That bright and fierce and fickle is the South,   5
And dark and true and tender is the North.

'O Swallow, Swallow, if I could follow, and light
Upon her lattice, I would pipe and trill,
And cheep and twitter twenty million loves.

'O were I thou that she might take me in,   10
And lay me on her bosom, and her heart
Would rock the snowy cradle till I died.

'Why lingereth she to clothe her heart with love,
Delaying as the tender ash delays
To clothe herself, when all the woods are green?   15

'O tell her, Swallow, that thy brood is flown:
Say to her, I do but wanton in the South,
But in the North long since my nest is made.

'O tell her, brief is life but love is long,
And brief the sun of summer in the North,   20
And brief the moon of beauty in the South.

'O Swallow, flying from the golden woods,
Fly to her, and pipe and woo her, and make her mine,
And tell her, tell her, that I follow thee.'

'NOW SLEEPS THE CRIMSON PETAL'

'Now sleeps the crimson petal, now the white;
Nor waves the cypress in the palace walk;
Nor winks the gold fin in the porphyry font:
The fire-fly wakens: waken thou with me.

Now droops the milkwhite peacock like a ghost,   5
And like a ghost she glimmers on to me.

Now lies the Earth all Danaë to the stars,
And all thy heart lies open unto me.

Now slides the silent meteor on, and leaves
A shining furrow, as thy thoughts in me.   10

Now folds the lily all her sweetness up,
And slips into the bosom of the lake:
So fold thyself, my dearest, thou, and slip
Into my bosom and be lost in me.'

'COME DOWN, O MAID'

'Come down, O maid, from yonder mountain height:
What pleasure lives in height (the shepherd sang)
In height and cold, the splendour of the hills?
But cease to move so near the Heavens, and cease
To glide a sunbeam by the blasted Pine,   5
To sit a star upon the sparkling spire;
And come, for Love is of the valley, come,
For Love is of the valley, come thou down
And find him; by the happy threshold, he,
Or hand in hand with Plenty in the maize,   10
Or red with spirted purple of the vats,
Or foxlike in the vine; nor cares to walk
With Death and Morning on the silver horns,
Nor wilt thou snare him in the white ravine,
Nor find him dropt upon the firths of ice,   15
That huddling slant in furrow-cloven falls
To roll the torrent out of dusky doors:
But follow; let the torrent dance thee down
To find him in the valley; let the wild
Lean-headed Eagles yelp alone, and leave   20
The monstrous ledges there to slope, and spill
Their thousand wreaths of dangling water-smoke,
That like a broken purpose waste in air:
So waste not thou; but come; for all the vales
Await thee; azure pillars of the hearth   25
Arise to thee; the children call, and I
Thy shepherd pipe, and sweet is every sound,
Sweeter thy voice, but every sound is sweet;
Myriads of rivulets hurrying thro' the lawn,
The moan of doves in immemorial elms,   30
And murmuring of innumerable bees.'

'THE SPLENDOUR FALLS'

[added in 3rd edn., 1850]

The splendour falls on castle walls
    And snowy summits old in story:
The long light shakes across the lakes,
    And the wild cataract leaps in glory.
Blow, bugle, blow, set the wild echoes flying,   5
Blow, bugle; answer, echoes, dying, dying, dying.

    O hark, O hear! how thin and clear,
        And thinner, clearer, farther going!
    O sweet and far from cliff and scar
        The horns of Elfland faintly blowing!   10
Blow, let us hear the purple glens replying:
Blow, bugle; answer, echoes, dying, dying, dying.

    O love, they die in yon rich sky,
        They faint on hill or field or river:
    Our echoes roll from soul to soul,   15
        And grow for ever and for ever.
Blow, bugle, blow, set the wild echoes flying,
And answer, echoes, answer, dying, dying, dying.

'ASK ME NO MORE'

[added in 3rd edn., 1850]

Ask me no more: the moon may draw the sea;
    The cloud may stoop from heaven and take the shape
    With fold to fold, of mountain or of cape;
But O too fond, when have I answer'd thee?
                Ask me no more.   5

Ask me no more: what answer should I give?
   I love not hollow cheek or faded eye:
   Yet, O my friend, I will not have thee die!
Ask me no more, lest I should bid thee live;
         Ask me no more.   10

Ask me no more: thy fate and mine are seal'd:
   I strove against the stream and all in vain:
   Let the great river take me to the main:
No more, dear love, for at a touch I yield;
         Ask me no more.   15

To—, After Reading a Life and Letters

Published 1849 (in the *Examiner*)

'Cursed be he that moves my bones.'
Shakespeare's Epitaph

YOU might have won the Poet's name,
   If such be worth the winning now,
   And gain'd a laurel for your brow
Of sounder leaf than I can claim;

But you have made the wiser choice,   5
   A life that moves to gracious ends
   Thro' troops of unrecording friends,
A deedful life, a silent voice:

And you have miss'd the irreverent doom
   Of those that wear the Poet's crown: 10
   Hereafter, neither knave nor clown
Shall hold their orgies at your tomb.

For now the Poet cannot die,
   Nor leave his music as of old,
   But round him ere he scarce be cold   15
Begins the scandal and the cry:

'Proclaim the faults he would not show:
   Break lock and seal: betray the trust:
   Keep nothing sacred: 'tis but just
The many-headed beast should know.'   20

Ah shameless! for he did but sing
   A song that pleased us from its worth;
   No public life was his on earth,
No blazon'd statesman he, nor king.

He gave the people of his best: 25
   His worst he kept, his best he gave.
   My Shakespeare's curse on clown and knave
Who will not let his ashes rest!

Who make it seem more sweet to be
   The little life of bank and brier,   30
   The bird that pipes his lone desire
And dies unheard within his tree,

Than he that warbles long and loud
   And drops at Glory's temple-gates,
   For whom the carrion vulture waits   35
To tear his heart before the crowd!

From In Memoriam A. H. H.

OBIIT MDCCCXXXIII

Published 1850

[PROLOGUE]

STRONG Son of God, immortal Love,
    Whom we, that have not seen thy face,
    By faith, and faith alone, embrace,
Believing where we cannot prove;

Thine are these orbs of light and shade;   5
    Thou madest Life in man and brute;
    Thou madest Death; and lo, thy foot
Is on the skull which thou hast made.

Thou wilt not leave us in the dust:
    Thou madest man, he knows not why,   10
    He thinks he was not made to die;
And thou hast made him: thou art just.

Thou seemest human and divine,
    The highest, holiest manhood, thou:
    Our wills are ours, we know not how;   15
Our wills are ours, to make them thine.

Our little systems have their day;
    They have their day and cease to be:
    They are but broken lights of thee,
And thou, O Lord, art more than they.   20

We have but faith: we cannot know;
    For knowledge is of things we see;
    And yet we trust it comes from thee,
A beam in darkness: let it grow.

Let knowledge grow from more to more,   25
   But more of reverence in us dwell;
   That mind and soul, according well,
May make one music as before,

But vaster. We are fools and slight;
   We mock thee when we do not fear: 30
   But help thy foolish ones to bear;
Help thy vain worlds to bear thy light.

Forgive what seem'd my sin in me;
   What seem'd my worth since I began;
   For merit lives from man to man,   35
And not from man, O Lord, to thee.

Forgive my grief for one removed,
   Thy creature, whom I found so fair.
   I trust he lives in thee, and there
I find him worthier to be loved.   40

Forgive these wild and wandering cries,
   Confusions of a wasted youth;
   Forgive them where they fail in truth,
And in thy wisdom make me wise.

                1849.

VII

Dark house, by which once more I stand
   Here in the long unlovely street,
   Doors, where my heart was used to beat
So quickly, waiting for a hand,

A hand that can be clasp'd no more—   5
   Behold me, for I cannot sleep,
   And like a guilty thing I creep
At earliest morning to the door.

He is not here; but far away
   The noise of life begins again,   10
   And ghastly thro' the drizzling rain
On the bald street breaks the blank day.

XI

Calm is the morn without a sound,
   Calm as to suit a calmer grief,
   And only thro' the faded leaf
The chestnut pattering to the ground:

Calm and deep peace on this high wold,   5
   And on these dews that drench the furze,
   And all the silvery gossamers
That twinkle into green and gold:

Calm and still light on yon great plain
   That sweeps with all its autumn bowers,   10
   And crowded farms and lessening towers,
To mingle with the bounding main:

Calm and deep peace in this wide air,
   These leaves that redden to the fall;
   And in my heart, if calm at all,   15
If any calm, a calm despair:

Calm on the seas, and silver sleep,
   And waves that sway themselves in rest,
   And dead calm in that noble breast
Which heaves but with the heaving deep.   20

XV

To-night the winds begin to rise
   And roar from yonder dropping day:
   The last red leaf is whirl'd away,
The rooks are blown about the skies;

The forest crack'd, the waters curl'd,　　　5
　　The cattle huddled on the lea;
　　And wildly dash'd on tower and tree
The sunbeam strikes along the world:

And but for fancies, which aver
　　That all thy motions gently pass　　　10
　　Athwart a plane of molten glass,
I scarce could brook the strain and stir

That makes the barren branches loud;
　　And but for fear it is not so,
　　The wild unrest that lives in woe　　　15
Would dote and pore on yonder cloud

That rises upward always higher,
　　And onward drags a labouring breast,
　　And topples round the dreary west,
A looming bastion fringed with fire.　　　20

XIX

The Danube to the Severn gave
　　The darken'd heart that beat no more;
　　They laid him by the pleasant shore,
And in the hearing of the wave.

There twice a day the Severn fills;　　　5
　　The salt sea-water passes by,
　　And hushes half the babbling Wye,
And makes a silence in the hills.

The Wye is hush'd nor moved along,
　　And hush'd my deepest grief of all,　　　10
　　When fill'd with tears that cannot fall,
I brim with sorrow drowning song.

The tide flows down, the wave again
    Is vocal in its wooded walls;
    My deeper anguish also falls,   15
And I can speak a little then.

XXXIV

My own dim life should teach me this,
    That life shall live for evermore,
    Else earth is darkness at the core,
And dust and ashes all that is;

This round of green, this orb of flame,   5
    Fantastic beauty; such as lurks
    In some wild Poet, when he works
Without a conscience or an aim.

What then were God to such as I?
    'Twere hardly worth my while to choose   10
    Of things all mortal, or to use
A little patience ere I die;

'Twere best at once to sink to peace,
    Like birds the charming serpent draws,
    To drop head-foremost in the jaws   15
Of vacant darkness and to cease.

XXXV

Yet if some voice that man could trust
    Should murmur from the narrow house,
    'The cheeks drop in; the body bows;
Man dies: nor is there hope in dust:'

Might I not say? 'Yet even here,   5
    But for one hour, O Love, I strive
    To keep so sweet a thing alive:'
But I should turn mine ears and hear

The moanings of the homeless sea,
 The sound of streams that swift or slow 10
 Draw down Æonian hills, and sow
The dust of continents to be;

And Love would answer with a sigh,
 'The sound of that forgetful shore
 Will change my sweetness more and more, 15
Half-dead to know that I shall die.'

O me, what profits it to put
 An idle case? If Death were seen
 At first as Death, Love had not been,
Or been in narrowest working shut, 20

Mere fellowship of sluggish moods,
 Or in his coarsest Satyr-shape
 Had bruised the herb and crush'd the grape,
And bask'd and batten'd in the woods.

L

Be near me when my light is low,
 When the blood creeps, and the nerves prick
 And tingle; and the heart is sick,
And all the wheels of Being slow.

Be near me when the sensuous frame 5
 Is rack'd with pangs that conquer trust;
 And Time, a maniac scattering dust,
And Life, a Fury slinging flame.

Be near me when my faith is dry,
 And men the flies of latter spring, 10
 That lay their eggs, and sting and sing
And weave their petty cells and die.

Be near me when I fade away,
   To point the term of human strife,
   And on the low dark verge of life   15
The twilight of eternal day.

LIV

Oh yet we trust that somehow good
   Will be the final goal of ill,
   To pangs of nature, sins of will,
Defects of doubt, and taints of blood;

That nothing walks with aimless feet;   5
   That not one life shall be destroy'd,
   Or cast as rubbish to the void,
When God hath made the pile complete;

That not a worm is cloven in vain;
   That not a moth with vain desire   10
   Is shrivell'd in a fruitless fire,
Or but subserves another's gain.

Behold, we know not anything;
   I can but trust that good shall fall
   At last—far off—at last, to all,   15
And every winter change to spring.

So runs my dream: but what am I?
   An infant crying in the night:
   An infant crying for the light:
And with no language but a cry.   20

LV

The wish, that of the living whole
   No life may fail beyond the grave,
   Derives it not from what we have
The likest God within the soul?

Are God and Nature then at strife,   5
  That Nature lends such evil dreams?
  So careful of the type she seems,
So careless of the single life;

That I, considering everywhere
  Her secret meaning in her deeds,
  And finding that of fifty seeds   10
She often brings but one to bear,

I falter where I firmly trod,
  And falling with my weight of cares
  Upon the great world's altar-stairs   15
That slope thro' darkness up to God,

I stretch lame hands of faith, and grope,
  And gather dust and chaff, and call
  To what I feel is Lord of all,
And faintly trust the larger hope.   20

LVI

'So careful of the type?' but no.
  From scarped cliff and quarried stone
  She cries, 'A thousand types are gone:
I care for nothing, all shall go.

'Thou makest thine appeal to me: 5
  I bring to life, I bring to death:
  The spirit does but mean the breath:
I know no more.' And he, shall he,

Man, her last work, who seem'd so fair,
  Such splendid purpose in his eyes,   10
  Who roll'd the psalm to wintry skies,
Who built him fanes of fruitless prayer,

Who trusted God was love indeed
   And love Creation's final law—
   Tho' Nature, red in tooth and claw   15
With ravine, shriek'd against his creed—

Who loved, who suffer'd countless ills,
   Who battled for the True, the Just,
   Be blown about the desert dust,
Or seal'd within the iron hills?   20

No more? A monster then, a dream,
   A discord. Dragons of the prime,
   That tare each other in their slime,
Were mellow music match'd with him.

O life as futile, then, as frail!   25
   O for thy voice to soothe and bless!
   What hope of answer, or redress?
Behind the veil, behind the veil.

LXVII

When on my bed the moonlight falls,
   I know that in thy place of rest
   By that broad water of the west,
There comes a glory on the walls;

Thy marble bright in dark appears,   5
   As slowly steals a silver flame
   Along the letters of thy name,
And o'er the number of thy years.

The mystic glory swims away;
   From off my bed the moonlight dies;   10
   And closing eaves of wearied eyes
I sleep till dusk is dipt in gray:

And then I know the mist is drawn
  A lucid veil from coast to coast,
  And in the dark church like a ghost   15
Thy tablet glimmers to the dawn.

LXXXVI

Sweet after showers, ambrosial air,
  That rollest from the gorgeous gloom
  Of evening over brake and bloom
And meadow, slowly breathing bare

The round of space, and rapt below   5
  Thro' all the dewy-tassell'd wood,
  And shadowing down the horned flood
In ripples, fan my brows and blow

The fever from my cheek, and sigh
  The full new life that feeds thy breath   10
  Throughout my frame, till Doubt and Death,
Ill brethren, let the fancy fly

From belt to belt of crimson seas
  On leagues of odour streaming far,
  To where in yonder orient star   15
A hundred spirits whisper 'Peace.'

XCV

By night we linger'd on the lawn,
  For underfoot the herb was dry;
  And genial warmth; and o'er the sky
The silvery haze of summer drawn;

And calm that let the tapers burn   5
  Unwavering: not a cricket chirr'd:
  The brook alone far-off was heard,
And on the board the fluttering urn:

And bats went round in fragrant skies,
   And wheel'd or lit the filmy shapes   10
   That haunt the dusk, with ermine capes
And woolly breasts and beaded eyes;

While now we sang old songs that peal'd
   From knoll to knoll, where, couch'd at ease,
   The white kine glimmer'd, and the trees   15
Laid their dark arms about the field.

But when those others, one by one,
   Withdrew themselves from me and night,
   And in the house light after light
Went out, and I was all alone,   20

A hunger seized my heart; I read
   Of that glad year which once had been,
   In those fall'n leaves which kept their green,
The noble letters of the dead:

And strangely on the silence broke   25
   The silent-speaking words, and strange
   Was love's dumb cry defying change
To test his worth; and strangely spoke

The faith, the vigour, bold to dwell
   On doubts that drive the coward back,   30
   And keen thro' wordy snares to track
Suggestion to her inmost cell.

So word by word, and line by line,
   The dead man touch'd me from the past,
   And all at once it seem'd at last   35
The living soul was flash'd on mine,

And mine in this was wound, and whirl'd
   About empyreal heights of thought,
   And came on that which is, and caught
The deep pulsations of the world,   40

Æonian music measuring out
   The steps of Time—the shocks of Chance—
   The blows of Death. At length my trance
Was cancell'd, stricken thro' with doubt.

Vague words! but ah, how hard to frame   45
   In matter-moulded forms of speech,
   Or ev'n for intellect to reach
Thro' memory that which I became:

Till now the doubtful dusk reveal'd
   The knolls once more where, couch'd at ease,   50
   The white kine glimmer'd, and the trees
Laid their dark arms about the field:

And suck'd from out the distant gloom
   A breeze began to tremble o'er
   The large leaves of the sycamore,   55
And fluctuate all the still perfume,

And gathering freshlier overhead,
   Rock'd the full-foliaged elms, and swung
   The heavy-folded rose, and flung
The lilies to and fro, and said   60

'The dawn, the dawn,' and died away;
   And East and West, without a breath,
   Mixt their dim lights, like life and death,
To broaden into boundless day.

CI

Unwatch'd, the garden bough shall sway,
　　The tender blossom flutter down,
　　Unloved, that beech will gather brown,
This maple burn itself away;

Unloved, the sun-flower, shining fair,　　　　　　5
　　Ray round with flames her disk of seed,
　　And many a rose-carnation feed
With summer spice the humming air;

Unloved, by many a sandy bar,
　　The brook shall babble down the plain,　　　10
　　At noon or when the lesser wain
Is twisting round the polar star;

Uncared for, gird the windy grove,
　　And flood the haunts of hern and crake;
　　Or into silver arrows break　　　　　　　　　15
The sailing moon in creek and cove;

Till from the garden and the wild
　　A fresh association blow,
　　And year by year the landscape grow
Familiar to the stranger's child;　　　　　　　20

As year by year the labourer tills
　　His wonted glebe, or lops the glades;
　　And year by year our memory fades
From all the circle of the hills.

CVI

Ring out, wild bells, to the wild sky,
　　The flying cloud, the frosty light:
　　The year is dying in the night;
Ring out, wild bells, and let him die.

Ring out the old, ring in the new,   5
   Ring, happy bells, across the snow:
   The year is going, let him go;
Ring out the false, ring in the true.

Ring out the grief that saps the mind,
   For those that here we see no more;   10
   Ring out the feud of rich and poor,
Ring in redress to all mankind.

Ring out a slowly dying cause,
   And ancient forms of party strife;
   Ring in the nobler modes of life,   15
With sweeter manners, purer laws.

Ring out the want, the care, the sin,
   The faithless coldness of the times;
   Ring out, ring out my mournful rhymes,
But ring the fuller minstrel in.   20

Ring out false pride in place and blood,
   The civic slander and the spite;
   Ring in the love of truth and right,
Ring in the common love of good.

Ring out old shapes of foul disease;   25
   Ring out the narrowing lust of gold;
   Ring out the thousand wars of old,
Ring in the thousand years of peace.

Ring in the valiant man and free,
   The larger heart, the kindlier hand;   30
   Ring out the darkness of the land,
Ring in the Christ that is to be.

CXV

Now fades the last long streak of snow,
  Now burgeons every maze of quick
  About the flowering squares, and thick
By ashen roots the violets blow.

Now rings the woodland loud and long,   5
  The distance takes a lovelier hue,
  And drown'd in yonder living blue
The lark becomes a sightless song.

Now dance the lights on lawn and lea,
  The flocks are whiter down the vale,   10
  And milkier every milky sail
On winding stream or distant sea;

Where now the seamew pipes, or dives
  In yonder greening gleam, and fly
  The happy birds, that change their sky   15
To build and brood; that live their lives

From land to land; and in my breast
  Spring wakens too; and my regret
  Becomes an April violet,
And buds and blossoms like the rest.   20

CXVI

Is it, then, regret for buried time
  That keenlier in sweet April wakes,
  And meets the year, and gives and takes
The colours of the crescent prime?

Not all: the songs, the stirring air,   5
  The life re-orient out of dust,
  Cry thro' the sense to hearten trust
In that which made the world so fair.

Not all regret: the face will shine
   Upon me, while I muse alone;   10
   And that dear voice, I once have known,
Still speak to me of me and mine:

Yet less of sorrow lives in me
   For days of happy commune dead;
   Less yearning for the friendship fled,   15
Than some strong bond which is to be.

CXXIII

There rolls the deep where grew the tree.
   O earth, what changes hast thou seen!
   There where the long street roars, hath been
The stillness of the central sea.

The hills are shadows, and they flow   5
   From form to form, and nothing stands;
   They melt like mist, the solid lands,
Like clouds they shape themselves and go.

But in my spirit will I dwell,
   And dream my dream, and hold it true;   10
   For tho' my lips may breathe adieu,
I cannot think the thing farewell.

CXXIV

That which we dare invoke to bless;
   Our dearest faith; our ghastliest doubt;
   He, They, One, All; within, without;
The Power in darkness whom we guess;

I found Him not in world or sun,   5
   Or eagle's wing, or insect's eye;
   Nor thro' the questions men may try,
The petty cobwebs we have spun:

If e'er when faith had fall'n asleep,
  I heard a voice 'believe no more'   10
  And heard an ever-breaking shore
That tumbled in the Godless deep;

A warmth within the breast would melt
  The freezing reason's colder part,
  And like a man in wrath the heart   15
Stood up and answer'd 'I have felt.'

No, like a child in doubt and fear:
  But that blind clamour made me wise;
  Then was I as a child that cries,
But, crying, knows his father near;   20

And what I am beheld again
  What is, and no man understands;
  And out of darkness came the hands
That reach thro' nature, moulding men.

CXXX

Thy voice is on the rolling air;
  I hear thee where the waters run;
  Thou standest in the rising sun,
And in the setting thou art fair.

What art thou then? I cannot guess;   5
  But tho' I seem in star and flower
  To feel thee some diffusive power,
I do not therefore love thee less:

My love involves the love before;
  My love is vaster passion now;   10
  Tho' mix'd with God and Nature thou,
I seem to love thee more and more.

Far off thou art, but ever nigh;
  I have thee still, and I rejoice;
  I prosper, circled with thy voice;   15
I shall not lose thee tho' I die.

The Eagle

Published 1851 (in 7th edn. of 1842 *Poems*)

FRAGMENT

HE clasps the crag with crooked hands;
Close to the sun in lonely lands,
Ring'd with the azure world, he stands.

The wrinkled sea beneath him crawls;
He watches from his mountain walls,   5
And like a thunderbolt he falls.

Ode on the Death of the
Duke of Wellington

Published 1852

I

BURY the Great Duke
  With an empire's lamentation,
Let us bury the Great Duke
  To the noise of the mourning of a mighty nation,
Mourning when their leaders fall,   5
Warriors carry the warrior's pall,
And sorrow darkens hamlet and hall.

II

Where shall we lay the man whom we deplore?
Here, in streaming London's central roar.
Let the sound of those he wrought for,   10
And the feet of those he fought for,
Echo round his bones for evermore.

III

Lead out the pageant: sad and slow,
As fits an universal woe,
Let the long long procession go,   15
And let the sorrowing crowd about it grow,
And let the mournful martial music blow;
The last great Englishman is low.

IV

Mourn, for to us he seems the last,
Remembering all his greatness in the Past.   20
No more in soldier fashion will he greet
With lifted hand the gazer in the street.
O friends, our chief state-oracle is mute:
Mourn for the man of long-enduring blood,
The statesman-warrior, moderate, resolute,   25
Whole in himself, a common good.
Mourn for the man of amplest influence,
Yet clearest of ambitious crime,
Our greatest yet with least pretence,
Great in council and great in war,   30
Foremost captain of his time,
Rich in saving common-sense,
And, as the greatest only are,
In his simplicity sublime.

O good gray head which all men knew,   35
O voice from which their omens all men drew,
O iron nerve to true occasion true,
O fall'n at length that tower of strength
Which stood four-square to all the winds that blew!
Such was he whom we deplore.   40
The long self-sacrifice of life is o'er.
The great World-victor's victor will be seen no more.

V

All is over and done:
Render thanks to the Giver,
England, for thy son.   45
Let the bell be toll'd.
Render thanks to the Giver,
And render him to the mould.
Under the cross of gold
That shines over city and river,   50
There he shall rest for ever
Among the wise and the bold.
Let the bell be toll'd:
And a reverent people behold
The towering car, the sable steeds: 55
Bright let it be with its blazon'd deeds,
Dark in its funeral fold.
Let the bell be toll'd:
And a deeper knell in the heart be knoll'd;
And the sound of the sorrowing anthem roll'd   60
Thro' the dome of the golden cross;
And the volleying cannon thunder his loss;
He knew their voices of old.
For many a time in many a clime

His captain's-ear has heard them boom   65
Bellowing victory, bellowing doom:
When he with those deep voices wrought,
Guarding realms and kings from shame;
With those deep voices our dead captain taught
The tyrant, and asserts his claim   70
In that dread sound to the great name,
Which he has worn so pure of blame,
In praise and in dispraise the same,
A man of well-attemper'd frame.
O civic muse, to such a name,   75
To such a name for ages long,
To such a name,
Preserve a broad approach of fame,
And ever-echoing avenues of song.

VI

Who is he that cometh, like an honour'd guest,   80
With banner and with music, with soldier and with
        priest,
With a nation weeping, and breaking on my rest?
Mighty Seaman, this is he
Was great by land as thou by sea.
Thine island loves thee well, thou famous man,   85
The greatest sailor since our world began.
Now, to the roll of muffled drums,
To thee the greatest soldier comes;
For this is he
Was great by land as thou by sea;   90
His foes were thine; he kept us free;
O give him welcome, this is he
Worthy of our gorgeous rites,
And worthy to be laid by thee;

For this is England's greatest son,   95
He that gain'd a hundred fights,
Nor ever lost an English gun;
This is he that far away
Against the myriads of Assaye
Clash'd with his fiery few and won;   100
And underneath another sun,
Warring on a later day,
Round affrighted Lisbon drew
The treble works, the vast designs
Of his labour'd rampart-lines,   105
Where he greatly stood at bay,
Whence he issued forth anew,
And ever great and greater grew,
Beating from the wasted vines
Back to France her banded swarms,   110
Back to France with countless blows,
Till o'er the hills her eagles flew
Beyond the Pyrenean pines,
Follow'd up in valley and glen
With blare of bugle, clamour of men,   115
Roll of cannon and clash of arms,
And England pouring on her foes.
Such a war had such a close.
Again their ravening eagle rose
In anger, wheel'd on Europe-shadowing wings,   120
And barking for the thrones of kings;
Till one that sought but Duty's iron crown
On that loud sabbath shook the spoiler down;
A day of onsets of despair!
Dash'd on every rocky square   125
Their surging charges foam'd themselves away;
Last, the Prussian trumpet blew;

Thro' the long-tormented air
Heaven flash'd a sudden jubilant ray,
And down we swept and charged and overthrew. 130
So great a soldier taught us there,
What long-enduring hearts could do
In that world-earthquake, Waterloo!
Mighty Seaman, tender and true,
And pure as he from taint of craven guile,   135
O saviour of the silver-coasted isle,
O shaker of the Baltic and the Nile,
If aught of things that here befall
Touch a spirit among things divine,
If love of country move thee there at all,   140
Be glad, because his bones are laid by thine!
And thro' the centuries let a people's voice
In full acclaim,
A people's voice,
The proof and echo of all human fame,   145
A people's voice, when they rejoice
At civic revel and pomp and game,
Attest their great commander's claim
With honour, honour, honour, honour to him,
Eternal honour to his name.   150

VII

A people's voice! we are a people yet.
Tho' all men else their nobler dreams forget,
Confused by brainless mobs and lawless Powers;
Thank Him who isled us here, and roughly set
His Briton in blown seas and storming showers,   155
We have a voice, with which to pay the debt
Of boundless love and reverence and regret
To those great men who fought, and kept it ours.

And keep it ours, O God, from brute control;
O Statesmen, guard us, guard the eye, the soul   160
Of Europe, keep our noble England whole,
And save the one true seed of freedom sown
Betwixt a people and their ancient throne,
That sober freedom out of which there springs
Our loyal passion for our temperate kings;   165
For, saving that, ye help to save mankind
Till public wrong be crumbled into dust,
And drill the raw world for the march of mind,
Till crowds at length be sane and crowns be just.
But wink no more in slothful overtrust.   170
Remember him who led your hosts;
He bad you guard the sacred coasts.
Your cannons moulder on the seaward wall;
His voice is silent in your council-hall
For ever; and whatever tempests lour   175
For ever silent; even if they broke
In thunder, silent; yet remember all
He spoke among you, and the Man who spoke;
Who never sold the truth to serve the hour,
Nor palter'd with Eternal God for power;   180
Who let the turbid streams of rumour flow
Thro' either babbling world of high and low;
Whose life was work, whose language rife
With rugged maxims hewn from life;
Who never spoke against a foe;   185
Whose eighty winters freeze with one rebuke
All great self-seekers trampling on the right:
Truth-teller was our England's Alfred named;
Truth-lover was our English Duke;
Whatever record leap to light   190
He never shall be shamed.

VIII

Lo, the leader in these glorious wars
Now to glorious burial slowly borne,
Follow'd by the brave of other lands,
He, on whom from both her open hands   195
Lavish Honour shower'd all her stars,
And affluent Fortune emptied all her horn.
Yea, let all good things await
Him who cares not to be great,
But as he saves or serves the state.   200
Not once or twice in our rough island-story,
The path of duty was the way to glory:
He that walks it, only thirsting
For the right, and learns to deaden
Love of self, before his journey closes,   205
He shall find the stubborn thistle bursting
Into glossy purples, which outredden
All voluptuous garden-roses.
Not once or twice in our fair island-story,
The path of duty was the way to glory: 210
He, that ever following her commands,
On with toil of heart and knees and hands,
Thro' the long gorge to the far light has won
His path upward, and prevail'd,
Shall find the toppling crags of Duty scaled   215
Are close upon the shining table-lands
To which our God Himself is moon and sun.
Such was he: his work is done.
But while the races of mankind endure,
Let his great example stand   220
Colossal, seen of every land,
And keep the soldier firm, the statesman pure:

Till in all lands and thro' all human story
The path of duty be the way to glory:
And let the land whose hearths he saved from shame 225
For many and many an age proclaim
At civic revel and pomp and game,
And when the long-illumined cities flame,
Their ever-loyal iron leader's fame,
With honour, honour, honour, honour to him, 230
Eternal honour to his name.

IX

Peace, his triumph will be sung
By some yet unmoulded tongue
Far on in summers that we shall not see:
Peace, it is a day of pain 235
For one about whose patriarchal knee
Late the little children clung:
O peace, it is a day of pain
For one, upon whose hand and heart and brain
Once the weight and fate of Europe hung. 240
Ours the pain, be his the gain!
More than is of man's degree
Must be with us, watching here
At this, our great solemnity.
Whom we see not we revere; 245
We revere, and we refrain
From talk of battles loud and vain,
And brawling memories all too free
For such a wise humility
As befits a solemn fane: 250
We revere, and while we hear
The tides of Music's golden sea
Setting toward eternity,

Uplifted high in heart and hope are we,
Until we doubt not that for one so true   255
There must be other nobler work to do
Than when he fought at Waterloo,
And Victor he must ever be.
For tho' the Giant Ages heave the hill
And break the shore, and evermore   260
Make and break, and work their will;
Tho' world on world in myriad myriads roll
Round us, each with different powers,
And other forms of life than ours,
What know we greater than the soul?   265
On God and Godlike men we build our trust.
Hush, the Dead March wails in the people's ears:
The dark crowd moves, and there are sobs and tears:
The black earth yawns: the mortal disappears;
Ashes to ashes, dust to dust;   270
He is gone who seem'd so great.—
Gone; but nothing can bereave him
Of the force he made his own
Being here, and we believe him
Something far advanced in State,   275
And that he wears a truer crown
Than any wreath that man can weave him.
Speak no more of his renown,
Lay your earthly fancies down,
And in the vast cathedral leave him.   280
God accept him, Christ receive him.

The Charge of the Light Brigade

Published 1854 (in the *Examiner*)

I

HALF a league, half a league,
  Half a league onward,
All in the valley of Death
  Rode the six hundred.
'Forward, the Light Brigade!   5
Charge for the guns!' he said:
Into the valley of Death
  Rode the six hundred.

II

'Forward, the Light Brigade!'
Was there a man dismay'd?   10
Not tho' the soldier knew
  Some one had blunder'd:
Their's not to make reply,
Their's not to reason why,
Their's but to do and die: 15
Into the valley of Death
  Rode the six hundred.

III

Cannon to right of them,
Cannon to left of them,
Cannon in front of them   20
  Volley'd and thunder'd;

Storm'd at with shot and shell,
Boldly they rode and well,
Into the jaws of Death,
Into the mouth of Hell   25
   Rode the six hundred.

IV

Flash'd all their sabres bare,
Flash'd as they turn'd in air
Sabring the gunners there,
Charging an army, while   30
   All the world wonder'd:
Plunged in the battery-smoke
Right thro' the line they broke;
Cossack and Russian
Reel'd from the sabre-stroke   35
   Shatter'd and sunder'd.
Then they rode back, but not
   Not the six hundred.

V

Cannon to right of them,
Cannon to left of them,   40
Cannon behind them
   Volley'd and thunder'd;
Storm'd at with shot and shell,
While horse and hero fell,
They that had fought so well   45
Came thro' the jaws of Death,
Back from the mouth of Hell,
All that was left of them,
   Left of six hundred.

VI

When can their glory fade?   50
O the wild charge they made!
  All the world wonder'd.
Honour the charge they made!
Honour the Light Brigade,
  Noble six hundred!   55

From Maud

Maud, and Other Poems (1855)

PART I

III

COLD and clear-cut face, why come you so cruelly meek,
Breaking a slumber in which all spleenful folly was drown'd,
Pale with the golden beam of an eyelash dead on the cheek,
Passionless, pale, cold face, star-sweet on a gloom profound;
Womanlike, taking revenge too deep for a transient wrong   5
Done but in thought to your beauty, and ever as pale as before
Growing and fading and growing upon me without a sound,
Luminous, gemlike, ghostlike, deathlike, half the night long
Growing and fading and growing, till I could bear it no
    more,
But arose, and all by myself in my own dark garden ground,
Listening now to the tide in its broad-flung shipwrecking
    roar,   11
Now to the scream of a madden'd beach dragg'd down by the
    wave,
Walk'd in a wintry wind by a ghastly glimmer, and found
The shining daffodil dead, and Orion low in his grave.

V

I

A voice by the cedar tree
In the meadow under the Hall!
She is singing an air that is known to me,
A passionate ballad gallant and gay,
A martial song like a trumpet's call! 5
Singing alone in the morning of life,
In the happy morning of life and of May,
Singing of men that in battle array,
Ready in heart and ready in hand,
March with banner and bugle and fife 10
To the death, for their native land.

II

Maud with her exquisite face,
And wild voice pealing up to the sunny sky,
And feet like sunny gems on an English green,
Maud in the light of her youth and her grace, 15
Singing of Death, and of Honour that cannot die,
Till I well could weep for a time so sordid and mean,
And myself so languid and base.

III

Silence, beautiful voice!
Be still, for you only trouble the mind 20
With a joy in which I cannot rejoice,
A glory I shall not find.

Still! I will hear you no more,
For your sweetness hardly leaves me a choice
But to move to the meadow and fall before   25
Her feet on the meadow grass, and adore,
Not her, who is neither courtly nor kind,
Not her, not her, but a voice.

XXII

I

Come into the garden, Maud,
    For the black bat, night, has flown,
Come into the garden, Maud,
    I am here at the gate alone;
And the woodbine spices are wafted abroad,   5
    And the musk of the rose is blown.

II

For a breeze of morning moves,
    And the planet of Love is on high,
Beginning to faint in the light that she loves
    On a bed of daffodil sky,   10
To faint in the light of the sun she loves,
    To faint in his light, and to die.

III

All night have the roses heard
    The flute, violin, bassoon;
All night has the casement jessamine stirr'd   15
    To the dancers dancing in tune;
Till a silence fell with the waking bird,
    And a hush with the setting moon.

IV

I said to the lily, 'There is but one
  With whom she has heart to be gay.   20
When will the dancers leave her alone?
  She is weary of dance and play.'
Now half to the setting moon are gone,
  And half to the rising day;
Low on the sand and loud on the stone   25
  The last wheel echoes away.

V

I said to the rose, 'The brief night goes
  In babble and revel and wine.
O young lord-lover, what sighs are those,
  For one that will never be thine?   30
But mine, but mine,' so I sware to the rose,
  'For ever and ever, mine.'

VI

And the soul of the rose went into my blood,
  As the music clash'd in the hall;
And long by the garden lake I stood,   35
  For I heard your rivulet fall
From the lake to the meadow and on to the wood,
  Our wood, that is dearer than all;

VII

From the meadow your walks have left so sweet
  That whenever a March-wind sighs   40
He sets the jewel-print of your feet
  In violets blue as your eyes,
To the woody hollows in which we meet
  And the valleys of Paradise.

VIII

The slender acacia would not shake   45
    One long milk-bloom on the tree;
The white lake-blossom fell into the lake
    As the pimpernel dozed on the lea;
But the rose was awake all night for your sake,
    Knowing your promise to me;   50
The lilies and roses were all awake,
    They sigh'd for the dawn and thee.

IX

Queen rose of the rosebud garden of girls,
    Come hither, the dances are done,
In gloss of satin and glimmer of pearls,   55
    Queen lily and rose in one;
Shine out, little head, sunning over with curls,
    To the flowers, and be their sun.

X

There has fallen a splendid tear
    From the passion-flower at the gate.   60
She is coming, my dove, my dear;
    She is coming, my life, my fate;
The red rose cries, 'She is near, she is near;'
    And the white rose weeps, 'She is late;'
The larkspur listens, 'I hear, I hear;'   65
    And the lily whispers, 'I wait.'

XI

She is coming, my own, my sweet;
    Were it ever so airy a tread,
My heart would hear her and beat,
    Were it earth in an earthy bed;   70

My dust would hear her and beat,
  Had I lain for a century dead;
Would start and tremble under her feet,
  And blossom in purple and red.

PART II

II

I

See what a lovely shell,
Small and pure as a pearl,
Lying close to my foot,
Frail, but a work divine,
Made so fairily well   5
With delicate spire and whorl,
How exquisitely minute,
A miracle of design!

II

What is it? a learned man
Could give it a clumsy name.   10
Let him name it who can,
The beauty would be the same.

III

The tiny cell is forlorn,
Void of the little living will
That made it stir on the shore.   15
Did he stand at the diamond door
Of his house in a rainbow frill?
Did he push, when he was uncurl'd,
A golden foot or a fairy horn
Thro' his dim water-world?   20

IV

Slight, to be crush'd with a tap
Of my finger-nail on the sand,
Small, but a work divine,
Frail, but of force to withstand,
Year upon year, the shock   25
Of cataract seas that snap
The three decker's oaken spine
Athwart the ledges of rock,
Here on the Breton strand!

.   .   .   .

IV

I

O that 'twere possible
After long grief and pain
To find the arms of my true love
Round me once again!

II

When I was wont to meet her   5
In the silent woody places
By the home that gave me birth,
We stood tranced in long embraces
Mixt with kisses sweeter sweeter
Than anything on earth.   10

III

A shadow flits before me,
Not thou, but like to thee:
Ah Christ, that it were possible
For one short hour to see
The souls we loved, that they might tell us   15
What and where they be.

IV

It leads me forth at evening,
It lightly winds and steals
In a cold white robe before me,
When all my spirit reels   20
At the shouts, the leagues of lights,
And the roaring of the wheels.

V

Half the night I waste in sighs,
Half in dreams I sorrow after
The delight of early skies;   25
In a wakeful doze I sorrow
For the hand, the lips, the eyes,
For the meeting of the morrow,
The delight of happy laughter,
The delight of low replies.   30

. . . . .

The Passing of Arthur

The Holy Grail, and Other Poems (1869: 1870 on title-page)

THAT story which the bold Sir Bedivere,
First made and latest left of all the knights,
Told, when the man was no more than a voice
In the white winter of his age, to those
With whom he dwelt, new faces, other minds.   5

For on their march to westward, Bedivere,
Who slowly paced among the slumbering host,
Heard in his tent the moanings of the King:

'I found Him in the shining of the stars,
I mark'd Him in the flowering of His fields,   10
But in His ways with men I find Him not.
I waged His wars, and now I pass and die.
O me! for why is all around us here
As if some lesser god had made the world,
But had not force to shape it as he would,   15
Till the High God behold it from beyond,
And enter it, and make it beautiful?
Or else as if the world were wholly fair,
But that these eyes of men are dense and dim,
And have not power to see it as it is: 20
Perchance, because we see not to the close;—
For I, being simple, thought to work His will,
And have but stricken with the sword in vain;
And all whereon I lean'd in wife and friend
Is traitor to my peace, and all my realm   25
Reels back into the beast, and is no more.
My God, thou hast forgotten me in my death:
Nay—God my Christ—I pass but shall not die.'

Then, ere that last weird battle in the west,
There came on Arthur sleeping, Gawain kill'd   30
In Lancelot's war, the ghost of Gawain blown
Along a wandering wind, and past his ear
Went shrilling, 'Hollow, hollow all delight!
Hail, King! to-morrow thou shalt pass away.
Farewell! there is an isle of rest for thee.   35
And I am blown along a wandering wind,
And hollow, hollow, hollow all delight.'
And fainter onward, like wild birds that change
Their season in the night and wail their way
From cloud to cloud, down the long wind the dream   40

Shrill'd; but in going mingled with dim cries
Far in the moonlit haze among the hills,
As of some lonely city sack'd by night,
When all is lost, and wife and child with wail
Pass to new lords; and Arthur woke and call'd,   45
'Who spake? A dream. O light upon the wind,
Thine, Gawain, was the voice—are these dim cries
Thine? or doth all that haunts the waste and wild
Mourn, knowing it will go along with me?'

This heard the bold Sir Bedivere and spake: 50
'O me, my King, let pass whatever will,
Elves, and the harmless glamour of the field;
But in their stead thy name and glory cling
To all high places like a golden cloud
For ever: but as yet thou shalt not pass.   55
Light was Gawain in life, and light in death
Is Gawain, for the ghost is as the man;
And care not thou for dreams from him, but rise—
I hear the steps of Modred in the west,
And with him many of thy people, and knights   60
Once thine, whom thou hast loved, but grosser grown
Than heathen, spitting at their vows and thee.
Right well in heart they know thee for the King.
Arise, go forth and conquer as of old.'

Then spake King Arthur to Sir Bedivere: 65
'Far other is this battle in the west
Whereto we move, than when we strove in youth,
And brake the petty kings, and fought with Rome,
Or thrust the heathen from the Roman wall,
And shook him thro' the north. Ill doom is mine   70
To war against my people and my knights.

The king who fights his people fights himself.
And they my knights, who loved me once, the stroke
That strikes them dead is as my death to me.
Yet let us hence, and find or feel a way   75
Thro' this blind haze, which ever since I saw
One lying in the dust at Almesbury,
Hath folded in the passes of the world.'

    Then rose the King and moved his host by night,
And ever push'd Sir Modred, league by league,   80
Back to the sunset bound of Lyonnesse—
A land of old upheaven from the abyss
By fire, to sink into the abyss again;
Where fragments of forgotten peoples dwelt,
And the long mountains ended in a coast   85
Of ever-shifting sand, and far away
The phantom circle of a moaning sea.
There the pursuer could pursue no more,
And he that fled no further fly the King;
And there, that day when the great light of heaven   90
Burn'd at his lowest in the rolling year,
On the waste sand by the waste sea they closed.
Nor ever yet had Arthur fought a fight
Like this last, dim, weird battle of the west.
A deathwhite mist slept over sand and sea: 95
Whereof the chill, to him who breathed it, drew
Down with his blood, till all his heart was cold
With formless fear; and ev'n on Arthur fell
Confusion, since he saw not whom he fought.
For friend and foe were shadows in the mist,   100
And friend slew friend not knowing whom he slew;
And some had visions out of golden youth,
And some beheld the faces of old ghosts

Look in upon the battle; and in the mist
Was many a noble deed, many a base,   105
And chance and craft and strength in single fights,
And ever and anon with host to host
Shocks, and the splintering spear, the hard mail hewn,
Shield-breakings, and the clash of brands, the crash
Of battleaxes on shatter'd helms, and shrieks   110
After the Christ, of those who falling down
Look'd up for heaven, and only saw the mist;
And shouts of heathen and the traitor knights,
Oaths, insult, filth, and monstrous blasphemies,
Sweat, writhings, anguish, labouring of the lungs   115
In that close mist, and cryings for the light,
Moans of the dying, and voices of the dead.

   Last, as by some one deathbed after wail
Of suffering, silence follows, or thro' death
Or deathlike swoon, thus over all that shore,   120
Save for some whisper of the seething seas,
A dead hush fell; but when the dolorous day
Grew drearier toward twilight falling, came
A bitter wind, clear from the North, and blew
The mist aside, and with that wind the tide   125
Rose, and the pale King glanced across the field
Of battle: but no man was moving there;
Nor any cry of Christian heard thereon,
Nor yet of heathen; only the wan wave
Brake in among dead faces, to and fro   130
Swaying the helpless hands, and up and down
Tumbling the hollow helmets of the fallen,
And shiver'd brands that once had fought with Rome,
And rolling far along the gloomy shores
The voice of days of old and days to be.   135

Then spake King Arthur to Sir Bedivere,
And whiter than the mist that all day long
Had held the field of battle was the King:

'Hearest thou this great voice that shakes the world,
And wastes the narrow realm whereon we move,   140
And beats upon the faces of the dead,
My dead, as tho' they had not died for me?—
O Bedivere, for on my heart hath fall'n
Confusion, till I know not what I am,
Nor whence I am, nor whether I be King.   145
Behold, I seem but King among the dead.'

Then spake the bold Sir Bedivere: 'My King,
King everywhere! and so the dead have kings,
There also will I worship thee as King.
Yet still thy life is whole, and still I live   150
Who love thee; but who hates thee, he that brought
The heathen back among us, yonder stands,
Modred, unharm'd, the traitor of thine house.'

Then spake the King: 'My house hath been my doom.
But call not thou this traitor of my house   155
Who hath but dwelt beneath one roof with me.
My house are rather they who sware my vows,
Yea, even while they brake them, own'd me King.
And well for thee, saying in my dark hour,
When all the purport of my throne hath fail'd,   160
That quick or dead thou holdest me for King.
King am I, whatsoever be their cry;
And one last act of kinghood shalt thou see
Yet, ere I pass.' And uttering this the King
Made at the man: then Modred smote his liege   165

Hard on that helm which many a heathen sword
Had beaten thin; while Arthur at one blow,
Striking the last stroke with Excalibur,
Slew him, and all but slain himself, he fell.

So all day long the noise of battle roll'd   170
Among the mountains by the winter sea;
Until King Arthur's Table, man by man,
Had fall'n in Lyonnesse about their lord,
King Arthur. Then, because his wound was deep,
The bold Sir Bedivere uplifted him,   175
And bore him to a chapel nigh the field,
A broken chancel with a broken cross,
That stood on a dark strait of barren land:
On one side lay the Ocean, and on one
Lay a great water, and the moon was full.   180

Then spake King Arthur to Sir Bedivere:
'The sequel of to-day unsolders all
The goodliest fellowship of famous knights
Whereof this world holds record. Such a sleep
They sleep—the men I loved. I think that we   185
Shall never more, at any future time,
Delight our souls with talk of knightly deeds,
Walking about the gardens and the halls
Of Camelot, as in the days that were.
I perish by this people which I made,—   190
Tho' Merlin sware that I should come again
To rule once more; but, let what will be, be,
I am so deeply smitten thro' the helm
That without help I cannot last till morn.
Thou therefore take my brand Excalibur,   195
Which was my pride: for thou rememberest how

In those old days, one summer noon, an arm
Rose up from out the bosom of the lake,
Clothed in white samite, mystic, wonderful,
Holding the sword—and how I row'd across   200
And took it, and have worn it, like a king;
And, wheresoever I am sung or told
In aftertime, this also shall be known:
But now delay not: take Excalibur,
And fling him far into the middle mere: 205
Watch what thou seëst, and lightly bring me word.'

To him replied the bold Sir Bedivere:
'It is not meet, Sir King, to leave thee thus,
Aidless, alone, and smitten thro' the helm—
A little thing may harm a wounded man;   210
Yet I thy hest will all perform at full,
Watch what I see, and lightly bring thee word.'

So saying, from the ruin'd shrine he stept,
And in the moon athwart the place of tombs,
Where lay the mighty bones of ancient men,   215
Old knights, and over them the sea-wind sang
Shrill, chill, with flakes of foam. He, stepping down
By zigzag paths, and juts of pointed rock,
Came on the shining levels of the lake.

There drew he forth the brand Excalibur,   220
And o'er him, drawing it, the winter moon,
Brightening the skirts of a long cloud, ran forth
And sparkled keen with frost against the hilt:
For all the haft twinkled with diamond sparks,
Myriads of topaz-lights, and jacinth-work   225
Of subtlest jewellery. He gazed so long
That both his eyes were dazzled as he stood,

This way and that dividing the swift mind,
In act to throw: but at the last it seem'd
Better to leave Excalibur conceal'd   230
There in the many-knotted waterflags,
That whistled stiff and dry about the marge.
So strode he back slow to the wounded King.

Then spake King Arthur to Sir Bedivere:
'Hast thou perform'd my mission which I gave?   235
What is it thou hast seen? or what hast heard?'

And answer made the bold Sir Bedivere:
'I heard the ripple washing in the reeds,
And the wild water lapping on the crag.'

To whom replied King Arthur, faint and pale: 240
'Thou hast betray'd thy nature and thy name,
Not rendering true answer, as beseem'd
Thy fëalty, nor like a noble knight:
For surer sign had follow'd, either hand,
Or voice, or else a motion of the mere.   245
This is a shameful thing for men to lie.
Yet now, I charge thee, quickly go again,
As thou art lief and dear, and do the thing
I bad thee, watch, and lightly bring me word.'

Then went Sir Bedivere the second time   250
Across the ridge, and paced beside the mere,
Counting the dewy pebbles, fix'd in thought;
But when he saw the wonder of the hilt,
How curiously and strangely chased, he smote
His palms together, and he cried aloud: 255

'And if indeed I cast the brand away,
Surely a precious thing, one worthy note,

Should thus be lost for ever from the earth,
Which might have pleased the eyes of many men.
What good should follow this, if this were done? 260
What harm, undone? Deep harm to disobey,
Seeing obedience is the bond of rule.
Were it well to obey then, if a king demand
An act unprofitable, against himself?
The King is sick, and knows not what he does. 265
What record, or what relic of my lord
Should be to aftertime, but empty breath
And rumours of a doubt? But were this kept,
Stored in some treasure-house of mighty kings,
Some one might show it at a joust of arms, 270
Saying, "King Arthur's sword, Excalibur,
Wrought by the lonely maiden of the Lake.
Nine years she wrought it, sitting in the deeps
Upon the hidden bases of the hills."
So might some old man speak in the aftertime 275
To all the people, winning reverence.
But now much honour and much fame were lost.'

So spake he, clouded with his own conceit,
And hid Excalibur the second time,
And so strode back slow to the wounded King. 280

Then spoke King Arthur, breathing heavily:
'What is it thou hast seen? or what hast heard?'

And answer made the bold Sir Bedivere:
'I heard the water lapping on the crag,
And the long ripple washing in the reeds.' 285

To whom replied King Arthur, much in wrath:
'Ah, miserable and unkind, untrue,

Unknightly, traitor-hearted! Woe is me!
Authority forgets a dying king,
Laid widow'd of the power in his eye   290
That bow'd the will. I see thee what thou art,
For thou, the latest-left of all my knights,
In whom should meet the offices of all,
Thou wouldst betray me for the precious hilt;
Either from lust of gold, or like a girl   295
Valuing the giddy pleasure of the eyes.
Yet, for a man may fail in duty twice,
And the third time may prosper, get thee hence:
But, if thou spare to fling Excalibur,
I will arise and slay thee with my hands.'   300

    Then quickly rose Sir Bedivere, and ran,
And, leaping down the ridges lightly, plunged
Among the bulrush beds, and clutch'd the sword,
And strongly wheel'd and threw it. The great brand
Made lightnings in the splendour of the moon,   305
And flashing round and round, and whirl'd in an arch,
Shot like a streamer of the northern morn,
Seen where the moving isles of winter shock
By night, with noises of the Northern Sea.
So flash'd and fell the brand Excalibur: 310
But ere he dipt the surface, rose an arm
Clothed in white samite, mystic, wonderful,
And caught him by the hilt, and brandish'd him
Three times, and drew him under in the mere.
And lightly went the other to the King.   315

    Then spoke King Arthur, drawing thicker breath:
'Now see I by thine eyes that this is done.
Speak out: what is it thou hast heard, or seen?'

And answer made the bold Sir Bedivere:
'Sir King, I closed mine eyelids, lest the gems   320
Should blind my purpose, for I never saw,
Nor shall see, here or elsewhere, till I die,
Not tho' I live three lives of mortal men,
So great a miracle as yonder hilt.
Then with both hands I flung him, wheeling him;   325
But when I look'd again, behold an arm,
Clothed in white samite, mystic, wonderful,
That caught him by the hilt, and brandish'd him
Three times, and drew him under in the mere.'

And answer made King Arthur, breathing hard: 330
'My end draws nigh; 'tis time that I were gone.
Make broad thy shoulders to receive my weight,
And bear me to the margin; yet I fear
My wound hath taken cold, and I shall die.'

So saying, from the pavement he half rose,   335
Slowly, with pain, reclining on his arm,
And looking wistfully with wide blue eyes
As in a picture. Him Sir Bedivere
Remorsefully regarded thro' his tears,
And would have spoken, but he found not words;   340
Then took with care, and kneeling on one knee,
O'er both his shoulders drew the languid hands,
And rising bore him thro' the place of tombs.

But, as he walk'd, King Arthur panted hard,
Like one that feels a nightmare on his bed   345
When all the house is mute. So sigh'd the King,
Muttering and murmuring at his ear, 'Quick, quick!
I fear it is too late, and I shall die.'

But the other swiftly strode from ridge to ridge,
Clothed with his breath, and looking, as he walk'd,   350
Larger than human on the frozen hills.
He heard the deep behind him, and a cry
Before. His own thought drove him like a goad.
Dry clash'd his harness in the icy caves
And barren chasms, and all to left and right   355
The bare black cliff clang'd round him, as he based
His feet on juts of slippery crag that rang
Sharp-smitten with the dint of armed heels—
And on a sudden, lo! the level lake,
And the long glories of the winter moon.   360

Then saw they how there hove a dusky barge,
Dark as a funeral scarf from stem to stern,
Beneath them; and descending they were ware
That all the decks were dense with stately forms,
Black-stoled, black-hooded, like a dream—by these   365
Three Queens with crowns of gold: and from them rose
A cry that shiver'd to the tingling stars,
And, as it were one voice, an agony
Of lamentation, like a wind that shrills
All night in a waste land, where no one comes,   370
Or hath come, since the making of the world.

Then murmur'd Arthur, 'Place me in the barge.'
So to the barge they came. There those three Queens
Put forth their hands, and took the King, and wept.
But she, that rose the tallest of them all   375
And fairest, laid his head upon her lap,
And loosed the shatter'd casque, and chafed his hands,
And call'd him by his name, complaining loud,
And dropping bitter tears against a brow

Striped with dark blood: for all his face was white   380
And colourless, and like the wither'd moon
Smote by the fresh beam of the springing east;
And all his greaves and cuisses dash'd with drops
Of onset; and the light and lustrous curls—
That made his forehead like a rising sun   385
High from the daïs-throne—were parch'd with dust;
Or, clotted into points and hanging loose,
Mix'd with the knightly growth that fringed his lips.
So like a shatter'd column lay the King;
Not like that Arthur who, with lance in rest,   390
From spur to plume a star of tournament,
Shot thro' the lists at Camelot, and charged
Before the eyes of ladies and of kings.

Then loudly cried the bold Sir Bedivere:
'Ah! my Lord Arthur, whither shall I go?   395
Where shall I hide my forehead and my eyes?
For now I see the true old times are dead,
When every morning brought a noble chance,
And every chance brought out a noble knight.
Such times have been not since the light that led   400
The holy Elders with the gift of myrrh.
But now the whole Round Table is dissolved
Which was an image of the mighty world,
And I, the last, go forth companionless,
And the days darken round me, and the years,   405
Among new men, strange faces, other minds.'

And slowly answer'd Arthur from the barge:
'The old order changeth, yielding place to new,
And God fulfils himself in many ways,
Lest one good custom should corrupt the world.   410

Comfort thyself: what comfort is in me?
I have lived my life, and that which I have done
May He within himself make pure! but thou,
If thou shouldst never see my face again,
Pray for my soul. More things are wrought by prayer 415
Than this world dreams of. Wherefore, let thy voice
Rise like a fountain for me night and day.
For what are men better than sheep or goats
That nourish a blind life within the brain,
If, knowing God, they lift not hands of prayer   420
Both for themselves and those who call them friend?
For so the whole round earth is every way
Bound by gold chains about the feet of God.
But now farewell. I am going a long way
With these thou seëst—if indeed I go   425
(For all my mind is clouded with a doubt)—
To the island-valley of Avilion;
Where falls not hail, or rain, or any snow,
Nor ever wind blows loudly; but it lies
Deep-meadow'd, happy, fair with orchard lawns   430
And bowery hollows crown'd with summer sea,
Where I will heal me of my grievous wound.'

   So said he, and the barge with oar and sail
Moved from the brink, like some full-breasted swan
That, fluting a wild carol ere her death,   435
Ruffles her pure cold plume, and takes the flood
With swarthy webs. Long stood Sir Bedivere
Revolving many memories, till the hull
Look'd one black dot against the verge of dawn,
And on the mere the wailing died away.   440

   But when that moan had past for evermore,
The stillness of the dead world's winter dawn

Amazed him, and he groan'd, 'The King is gone.'
And therewithal came on him the weird rhyme,
'From the great deep to the great deep he goes.'   445

Whereat he slowly turn'd and slowly clomb
The last hard footstep of that iron crag;
Thence mark'd the black hull moving yet, and cried,
'He passes to be King among the dead,
And after healing of his grievous wound   450
He comes again; but—if he come no more—
O me, be yon dark Queens in yon black boat,
Who shriek'd and wail'd, the three whereat we gazed
On that high day, when, clothed with living light,
They stood before his throne in silence, friends   455
Of Arthur, who should help him at his need?'

Then from the dawn it seem'd there came, but faint
As from beyond the limit of the world,
Like the last echo born of a great cry,
Sounds, as if some fair city were one voice   460
Around a king returning from his wars.

Thereat once more he moved about, and clomb
Ev'n to the highest he could climb, and saw,
Straining his eyes beneath an arch of hand,
Or thought he saw, the speck that bare the King,   465
Down that long water opening on the deep
Somewhere far off, pass on and on, and go
From less to less and vanish into light.
And the new sun rose bringing the new year.

'Flower in the Crannied Wall'

The Holy Grail, and Other Poems (1869)

FLOWER in the crannied wall,
I pluck you out of the crannies,
I hold you here, root and all, in my hand,
Little flower—but *if* I could understand
What you are, root and all, and all in all,   5
I should know what God and man is.

In the Garden at Swainston

Published 1874 (in the Cabinet Edition of Tennyson's poems)

NIGHTINGALES warbled without,
    Within was weeping for thee:
Shadows of three dead men
    Walk'd in the walks with me,
    Shadows of three dead men and thou wast one of the three. 5

Nightingales sang in his woods:
    The Master was far away:
Nightingales warbled and sang
    Of a passion that lasts but a day;
    Still in the house in his coffin the Prince of courtesy lay.   10

Two dead men have I known
    In courtesy like to thee:
Two dead men have I loved
    With a love that ever will be:
    Three dead men have I loved and thou art last of the
        three.   15

To Virgil

WRITTEN AT THE REQUEST OF THE MANTUANS FOR THE NINETEENTH CENTENARY OF VIRGIL'S DEATH

Published 1882 (in *The Nineteenth Century*)

I

ROMAN VIRGIL, thou that singest
    Ilion's lofty temples robed in fire,
Ilion falling, Rome arising,
    wars, and filial faith, and Dido's pyre;

II

Landscape-lover, lord of language   5
    more than he that sang the Works and Days,
All the chosen coin of fancy
    flashing out from many a golden phrase;

III

Thou that singest wheat and woodland,
    tilth and vineyard, hive and horse and herd;   10
All the charm of all the Muses
    often flowering in a lonely word;

IV

Poet of the happy Tityrus
    piping underneath his beechen bowers;
Poet of the poet-satyr   15
    whom the laughing shepherd bound with flowers;

V

Chanter of the Pollio, glorying
    in the blissful years again to be,
Summers of the snakeless meadow,
    unlaborious earth and oarless sea;   20

VI

Thou that seëst Universal
    Nature moved by Universal Mind;
Thou majestic in thy sadness
    at the doubtful doom of human kind;

VII

Light among the vanish'd ages;   25
    star that gildest yet this phantom shore;
Golden branch amid the shadows,
    kings and realms that pass to rise no more;

VIII

Now thy Forum roars no longer,
    fallen every purple Cæsar's dome—   30
Tho' thine ocean-roll of rhythm
    sound for ever of Imperial Rome—

IX

Now the Rome of slaves hath perish'd,
    and the Rome of freemen holds her place,
I, from out the Northern Island   35
    sunder'd once from all the human race,

X

I salute thee, Mantovano,
    I that loved thee since my day began,
Wielder of the stateliest measure
      ever moulded by the lips of man.   40

'Frater Ave Atque Vale'

Published 1883 (in *The Nineteenth Century*)

ROW us out from Desenzano, to your Sirmione row!
So they row'd, and there we landed—'O venusta Sirmio!'
There to me thro' all the groves of olive in the summer glow,
There beneath the Roman ruin where the purple flowers grow,
Came that 'Ave atque Vale' of the Poet's hopeless woe,   5
Tenderest of Roman poets nineteen-hundred years ago,
'Frater Ave atque Vale'—as we wander'd to and fro
Gazing at the Lydian laughter of the Garda Lake below
Sweet Catullus's all-but-island, olive-silvery Sirmio!

Rizpah

17—

Ballads and Other Poems (1880)

I

WAILING, wailing, wailing, the wind over land and sea—
And Willy's voice in the wind, 'O mother, come out to me.'
Why should he call me to-night, when he knows that I cannot
    go?
For the downs are as bright as day, and the full moon stares at
    the snow.

II

We should be seen, my dear; they would spy us out of the
town.   5
The loud black nights for us, and the storm rushing over the
down,
When I cannot see my own hand, but am led by the creak of
the chain,
And grovel and grope for my son till I find myself drenched
with the rain.

III

Anything fallen again? nay—what was there left to fall?
I have taken them home, I have number'd the bones, I have
hidden them all.   10
What am I saying? and what are *you*? do you come as a spy?
Falls? what falls? who knows? As the tree falls so must it lie.

IV

Who let her in? how long has she been? you—what have you
heard?
Why did you sit so quiet? you never have spoken a word.
O—to pray with me—yes—a lady—none of their spies—   15
But the night has crept into my heart, and begun to darken
my eyes.

V

Ah—you, that have lived so soft, what should *you* know of
the night,
The blast and the burning shame and the bitter frost and the
fright?
I have done it, while you were asleep—you were only made
for the day.
I have gather'd my baby together—and now you may go your
way.   20

VI

Nay—for it's kind of you, Madam, to sit by an old dying wife.

But say nothing hard of my boy, I have only an hour of life.

I kiss'd my boy in the prison, before he went out to die.

'They dared me to do it,' he said, and he never has told me a lie.

I whipt him for robbing an orchard once when he was but a child—   25

'The farmer dared me to do it,' he said; he was always so wild—

And idle—and couldn't be idle—my Willy—he never could rest.

The King should have made him a soldier, he would have been one of his best.

VII

But he lived with a lot of wild mates, and they never would let him be good;

They swore that he dare not rob the mail, and he swore that he would;   30

And he took no life, but he took one purse, and when all was done

He flung it among his fellows—I'll none of it, said my son.

VIII

I came into court to the Judge and the lawyers. I told them my tale,

God's own truth—but they kill'd him, they kill'd him for robbing the mail.

They hang'd him in chains for a show—we had always borne a good name—   35

To be hang'd for a thief—and then put away—isn't that enough shame?

Dust to dust—low down—let us hide! but they set him so
  high
That all the ships of the world could stare at him, passing by.
God 'ill pardon the hell-black raven and horrible fowls of the
  air,
But not the black heart of the lawyer who kill'd him and
  hang'd him there.   40

IX

And the jailer forced me away. I had bid him my last good-
  bye;
They had fasten'd the door of his cell. 'O mother!' I heard
  him cry.
I couldn't get back tho' I tried, he had something further to say,
And now I never shall know it. The jailer forced me away.

X

Then since I couldn't but hear that cry of my boy that was
  dead,   45
They seized me and shut me up: they fasten'd me down on my
  bed.
'Mother, O mother!'—he call'd in the dark to me year after
  year—
They beat me for that, they beat me—you know that I
  couldn't but hear;
And then at the last they found I had grown so stupid and still
They let me abroad again—but the creatures had worked their
  will.   50

XI

Flesh of my flesh was gone, but bone of my bone was left—
I stole them all from the lawyers—and you, will you call it
  a theft?—

My baby, the bones that had suck'd me, the bones that had
    laughed and had cried—
Theirs? O no! they are mine—not theirs—they had moved in
    my side.

XII

Do you think I was scared by the bones? I kiss'd 'em, I buried
    'em all—   55
I can't dig deep, I am old—in the night by the churchyard
    wall.
My Willy 'ill rise up whole when the trumpet of judgment
    'ill sound,
But I charge you never to say that I laid him in holy ground.

XIII

They would scratch him up—they would hang him again on
    the cursed tree.
Sin? O yes—we are sinners, I know—let all that be,   60
And read me a Bible verse of the Lord's good will toward
    men—
'Full of compassion and mercy, the Lord'—let me hear it
    again;
'Full of compassion and mercy—long-suffering.' Yes, O yes!
For the lawyer is born but to murder—the Saviour lives but to
    bless.
He'll never put on the black cap except for the worst of the
    worst,   65
And the first may be last—I have heard it in church—and the
    last may be first.
Suffering—O long-suffering—yes, as the Lord must know,
Year after year in the mist and the wind and the shower and
    the snow.

XIV

Heard, have you? what? they have told you he never repented his sin.

How do they know it? are *they* his mother? are *you* of his kin?   70

Heard! have you ever heard, when the storm on the downs began,

The wind that 'ill wail like a child and the sea that 'ill moan like a man?

XV

Election, Election and Reprobation—it's all very well.

But I go to-night to my boy, and I shall not find him in Hell.

For I cared so much for my boy that the Lord has look'd into my care,   75

And He means me I'm sure to be happy with Willy, I know not where.

XVI

And if *he* be lost—but to save *my* soul, that is all your desire:

Do you think that I care for *my* soul if my boy be gone to the fire?

I have been with God in the dark—go, go, you may leave me alone—

You never have borne a child—you are just as hard as a stone.   80

XVII

Madam, I beg your pardon! I think that you mean to be kind,

But I cannot hear what you say for my Willy's voice in the wind—

The snow and the sky so bright—he used but to call in the dark,
And he calls to me now from the church and not from the
    gibbet—for hark!
Nay—you can hear it yourself—it is coming—shaking the
    walls—   85
Willy—the moon's in a cloud——Good-night. I am going.
    He calls.

Vastness

Published 1885 (in *The Nineteenth Century*)

I

MANY a hearth upon our dark globe sighs after many a
    vanish'd face,
Many a planet by many a sun may roll with the dust of a
    vanish'd race.

II

Raving politics, never at rest—as this poor earth's pale history
    runs,—
What is it all but a trouble of ants in the gleam of a million
    million of suns?

III

Lies upon this side, lies upon that side, truthless violence
    mourn'd by the Wise,   5
Thousands of voices drowning his own in a popular torrent
    of lies upon lies;

IV

Stately purposes, valour in battle, glorious annals of army and
    fleet,
Death for the right cause, death for the wrong cause, trumpets
    of victory, groans of defeat;

V

Innocence seethed in her mother's milk, and Charity setting
    the martyr aflame;
Thraldom who walks with the banner of Freedom, and recks
    not to ruin a realm in her name.   10

VI

Faith at her zenith, or all but lost in the gloom of doubts that
    darken the schools;
Craft with a bunch of all-heal in her hand, follow'd up by her
    vassal legion of fools;

VII

Trade flying over a thousand seas with her spice and her vin-
    tage, her silk and her corn;
Desolate offing, sailorless harbours, famishing populace,
    wharves forlorn;

VIII

Star of the morning, Hope in the sunrise; gloom of the even-
    ing, Life at a close;   15
Pleasure who flaunts on her wide down-way with her flying
    robe and her poison'd rose;

IX

Pain, that has crawl'd from the corpse of Pleasure, a worm
    which writhes all day, and at night
Stirs up again in the heart of the sleeper, and stings him back
    to the curse of the light;

X

Wealth with his wines and his wedded harlots; honest Poverty,
    bare to the bone;
Opulent Avarice, lean as Poverty; Flattery gilding the rift in
    a throne;   20

XI

Fame blowing out from her golden trumpet a jubilant challenge to Time and to Fate;

Slander, her shadow, sowing the nettle on all the laurel'd graves of the Great;

XII

Love for the maiden, crown'd with marriage, no regrets for aught that has been,

Household happiness, gracious children, debtless competence, golden mean;

XIII

National hatreds of whole generations, and pigmy spites of the village spire;   25

Vows that will last to the last death-ruckle, and vows that are snapt in a moment of fire;

XIV

He that has lived for the lust of the minute, and died in the doing it, flesh without mind;

He that has nail'd all flesh to the Cross, till Self died out in the love of his kind;

XV

Spring and Summer and Autumn and Winter, and all these old revolutions of earth;

All new-old revolutions of Empire—change of the tide—what is all of it worth?   30

XVI

What the philosophies, all the sciences, poesy, varying voices of prayer?

All that is noblest, all that is basest, all that is filthy with all that is fair?

XVII

What is it all, if we all of us end but in being our own corpse-
   coffins at last,
Swallow'd in Vastness, lost in Silence, drown'd in the deeps of
   a meaningless Past?

XVIII

What but a murmur of gnats in the gloom, or a moment's
   anger of bees in their hive?—   35

   ★   ★   ★   ★

Peace, let it be! for I loved him, and love him for ever: the
   dead are not dead but alive.

Crossing the Bar

Demeter and Other Poems (1889)

SUNSET and evening star,
   And one clear call for me!
And may there be no moaning of the bar,
   When I put out to sea,

But such a tide as moving seems asleep,   5
   Too full for sound and foam,
When that which drew from out the boundless deep
   Turns again home.

Twilight and evening bell,
   And after that the dark!   10
And may there be no sadness of farewell,
   When I embark;

For tho' from out our bourne of Time and Place
   The flood may bear me far,
I hope to see my Pilot face to face   15
   When I have crost the bar.

NOTES TO THE POEMS

Note: Where no other source is given, all quotations by Tennyson and Hallam Tennyson are taken from their annotations to the Eversley edition of the poems. The comments by Sir Charles Tennyson are taken from his selection, *Poems of Alfred, Lord Tennyson* (London, 1954), those by A. C. Bradley from his *Commentary on In Memoriam* (London, 1901).

PAGE 54. MARIANA. 'The *moated grange* was no particular grange, but one which rose to the music of Shakespeare's words: "There, at the moated grange, resides this rejected Mariana" (*Measure for Measure*, Act III, Sc. i.)' (Tennyson).

4. *pear*: 'Altered from "peach", because "peach" spoils the desolation of the picture' (Tennyson).

PAGE 57. THE DYING SWAN. There is a legend that swans sing only once, at the moment before death.

26. *coronach*: Gaelic funeral-song or dirge.

PAGE 58. FATIMA. The poem was first given its present title in *Poems* (1842); in *Poems* (1832) it was called 'O Love, Love, Love!'

PAGE 60. THE LADY OF SHALOTT. See Introduction, p. 26.

69–72. According to Hallam Tennyson, 'The key to this tale of magic symbolism is of deep human significance and is to be found in [these] lines.'

76. *greaves*: leg-armour.

87. *baldric*: a belt, hung from one shoulder to the opposite hip, used to carry a sword or bugle.

PAGE 66. OENONE. Hallam Tennyson notes that the poem was influenced by the scenery of the Pyrenees and that it was partly written in the valley of Cauterez during Tennyson's visit there with Hallam in 1830. In Greek mythology Oenone was a nymph of Mount Ida, near Troy. She was loved and later deserted by Paris (the son of Priam, King of Troy) who had been exposed on Mount Ida as a child, because of a prophecy that he would bring ruin on Troy. He was subsequently brought up by shepherds.

10. *topmost Gargarus*: the highest mountain in the Ida range.

13. *Troas*: the region around Troy; *Ilion*: the Greek name for Troy itself.

28–29. *the golden bee Is lily-cradled*: this piece of natural history may not be entirely fanciful. The editors of *The Field* (vol. 217, 27 April 1961, p. 812) note that it is 'unusual, but not unknown' for bees to be trapped in flowers overnight. Tennyson may have found the idea in Marvell's *Upon Appleton House*, ll. 317–19.

39–40. These lines refer to the legend that the walls of Troy rose into place to the sound of Apollo's harp.

51. *reedy Simois*: one of the rivers of Troy.

65. *Hesperian gold*: from the garden of the Hesperides.

72. *Oread*: the Oreads were the nymphs of the mountains and the grottoes.

74. *married brows*: 'meeting eye-brows' (Tennyson).

79. *the halls of Peleus*: the only immortal not invited to the wedding of Peleus and Thetis was Eris, or Discord, who revenged herself by throwing among the guests a golden apple inscribed 'For the fairest'. Herè (Hera, wife of Zeus), Pallas Athene (goddess of wisdom), and Aphrodite (goddess of love) all claimed the apple, and Zeus decreed that the choice be left to a mortal, Paris.

81. *Iris*: goddess of the rainbow and messenger of the gods.

95. *amaracus*: 'marjoram' (Tennyson); *asphodel*: the flower with which the Elysian fields were said to be covered.

102. *peacock*: an emblem of Hera.

170–1. *Idalian . . . Paphian*: 'Idalium and Paphos in Cyprus are sacred to Aphrodite' (Tennyson).

220. *The Abominable*: Eris. See notes to l. 79.

259. *Cassandra*: the daughter of Priam. Because Apollo loved her he gave her the gift of prophecy, which enabled her to foresee the fall of Troy, but because she resisted him he decreed that no one should take notice of her prophecies.

PAGE 75. THE LOTOS-EATERS. In the ninth book of the *Odyssey* Homer tells how Odysseus (Ulysses), returning from Troy, comes to the land of the Lotos-eaters. Once his men have eaten the fruit they lose all longing for home, content to stay where they are for the rest of their lives.

23. *galingale*: an aromatic root.

133. *amaranth*: a legendary flower that never fades; *moly*: a magical plant with a white flower and a black root.

170. *asphodel*: see 'Oenone' l. 9, and note.

PAGE 81. ST. SIMEON STYLITES. St. Simeon lived from A.D. 390 to

NOTES

459. At the age of 30, after being expelled from his monastery for his extreme austerities, Simeon built a pillar, six feet high, and lived on it. During the next ten years he built new pillars until he made one sixty feet high, and on this he lived for thirty years without ever descending. His disciples brought his food by ladder and from the pillar he preached to large crowds.

169. *Abaddon*: the angel of the bottomless pit, Apollyon (see Revelation ix. 11); *Asmodeus*: the king of demons, sometimes identified with Apollyon.

208. *spikenard*: an aromatic ointment.

PAGE 88. ULYSSES. See Introduction, pp. 27–29. The poem is based not on the *Odyssey*, in which Ulysses' companions all perish, but on Dante's *Inferno*, Canto xxvi, in which Ulysses tells how he set off again with a single ship in search of fresh adventures. In the *Inferno* Ulysses is being punished for his cunning and trickery, which culminated in the stratagem of the Wooden Horse by which Troy was overthrown, but there is no mention of this in Tennyson's poem.

10. *Hyades*: the nymphs who gave moisture to the earth. They became stars in the sky, and when they rose at the same time as the sun wet weather was expected to follow.

63. *the Happy Isles*: the Islands of the Blest, Elysium.

PAGE 90. TITHONUS. Tithonus, son of Laomedon and brother of Priam, was loved by Eos, goddess of the dawn. She persuaded Zeus to make Tithonus immortal but forgot to ask for him to be made eternally young. Tithonus grew steadily older and feebler until the gods at last took pity on him and changed him into a grasshopper.

63. *Ilion . . . rose into towers*: cf. 'Oenone', ll. 39–40, and note.

PAGE 93. LOCKSLEY HALL. ' "Locksley Hall" is an imaginary place (tho' the coast is Lincolnshire) and the hero is imaginary. The whole poem represents young life, its good side, its deficiences, and its yearnings' (Tennyson: *Memoir*, i. 195). The narrator of the poem has been rejected by his cousin Amy in favour of a man for whom he has the deepest contempt.

155. *Mahratta-battle*: the princes of Indore, Gwalior, and the other Mahratta states of central India conducted several wars against the British in the late eighteenth and early nineteenth centuries.

180. *Joshua's moon*: see Joshua x. 12.

182 *the ringing grooves of change*: 'When I went by the first train

from Liverpool to Manchester (1830), I thought that the wheels ran in a groove. It was a black night and there was such a vast crowd round the train at the station that we could not see the wheels. Then I made this line' (Tennyson: *Memoir*, i. 195).

187. *crescent*: growing.

PAGE 104. THE TWO VOICES. Hallam Tennyson notes that the poem, dated 1833, had the alternative title *Thoughts of a Suicide* and 'was begun under the cloud of his overwhelming sorrow after the death of Arthur Hallam, which, as my father told me, for a while blotted out all joy from his life, and made him long for death'.

39. *thy deficiency*: i.e. your absence, the lack of you.

61–62. Cf. Marlowe, *Tamburlaine the Great, Part One*, II. vii. 24–25.

186. *cope*: top (cf. the coping-stones of a wall).

192. *fold*: cloud.

193. *oblique*: Tennyson notes, 'Our grandfathers said "obleege", which is now *oblīge*; in the same way I pronounce "oblique" *oblīque*.' Tennyson wanted 'oblique' to rhyme in the stanza with 'strike' and 'like', but, as F. L. Lucas observes, 'The reader is not likely to increase his enjoyment of Tennyson's poetry by doing his own ear such violence' (*Tennyson: Poetry and Prose*, p. 171).

195. *Ixion-like*: Ixion fell in love with Hera, the wife of Zeus, and embraced a cloud which Zeus had formed in Hera's likeness. As a punishment Ixion was bound to a perpetually turning fiery wheel.

219–25. A reference to the martyrdom of St. Stephen (Acts vii. 55).

228. *The elements were kindlier mix'd*: 'Some have happier dispositions' (Tennyson).

277. *The simple senses crown'd his head*: i.e. the senses, in the simplicity of their limited comprehension, acknowledged Death as king.

278. *Omega*: the final letter of the Greek alphabet.

325–6. A reference to the growth of bones in the embryo.

346–8. This allusion to the idea of reincarnation is developed further in the following stanza.

350. *Lethe*: a river in Hades, the realm of the dead; a draught of its waters brought oblivion to souls about to be reincarnated, so that they forgot their previous existence.

436. *Aeolian harp*: in Roman mythology, Aeolus was the god of the winds. An Aeolian harp is an instrument in which sounds are produced by the natural movement of air currents over the strings.

PAGE 121. WILL WATERPROOF'S LYRICAL MONOLOGUE. Hallam Tennyson quotes Edward FitzGerald: 'The "plump Head-waiter of The Cock", by Temple Bar [London], famous for chop and porter, was rather offended when told of this poem. "Had Mr. Tennyson dined oftener there, he would not have minded it so much," he said.'

8. *Lusitanian*: Lusitania was the classical name for Portugal.

61. *raffs*: 'scraps' (Tennyson).

PAGE 124. THE VISION OF SIN.

3. *a horse with wings*: Pegasus, the winged horse of Greek mythology, is often used as a symbol for poetry.

78. *my youth was half divine*: the speaker is the same person as the 'youth' of the opening section.

207–24. Tennyson observed that in this final section 'we see the land-scape which symbolizes God, Law and the future life'.

PAGE 132. 'BREAK, BREAK, BREAK'. 'This poem first saw the light along with the dawn in a Lincolnshire lane at 5 o'clock in the morning' (Tennyson). It is a poem of grief for Arthur Hallam.

PAGE 132. 'TEARS, IDLE TEARS'. Tennyson observes that the poem was written in the autumn at Tintern Abbey and that it conveys 'the sense of the abiding in the transient'.

PAGE 134. 'NOW SLEEPS THE CRIMSON PETAL'.

3. *porphyry*: a beautiful red stone of extreme hardness.

7. 'Zeus came down to Danaë . . . in a shower of golden stars' (Tennyson).

PAGE 135. 'COME DOWN, O MAID'. Hallam Tennyson notes that the poem was written in Switzerland, chiefly at Lauterbrunnen and Grindel-wald, and that 'For simple rhythm and vowel music my father con-sidered this Idyllic song . . . as among his most successful work.'

PAGE 136. 'THE SPLENDOUR FALLS'. Tennyson tells us that this song 'was written after hearing the echoes at Killarney in 1848. When I was there I heard a bugle blown beneath the "Eagle's Nest", and eight distinct echoes.'

PAGE 137. 'TO—'. According to Hallam Tennyson, 'My father was in-dignant that Keats' wild love-letters should have been published; but he said that he did not wish the public to think that the poem had been written with any particular reference to *Letters and Literary Remains of Keats* (published in 1848), by Lord Houghton.' Since Tennyson's poem was published in 1849, however, Lord Houghton's volume is generally thought to have been the occasion of it.

PAGE 139. IN MEMORIAM. PROLOGUE. This is in the nature of an apologia for the whole poem and was added in 1849 when Tennyson was considering publication.

19. *broken lights*: refracted rays.

28. *as before*: 'as in the ages of faith' (Tennyson).

33–34. Forgive me equally for doing what I thought was wrong and what I thought was right [for I may have been mistaken in either case].

VII. 1. *Dark house*: Hallam's house, 67 Wimpole Street, London.

XI. The scene is Lincolnshire. The poet looks from the high land of the wold across the flat land to the sea in the distance; the ship he sees sailing there reminds him of the ship which is bringing Hallam's body home to England.

2. *calmer*: i.e. than Tennyson's.

7–8. The image is of the sun catching the dew-drops on the spiders' webs ('gossamers').

12. *bounding main*: the sea forms the limit of the scene.

XV. 9–11. His imagination tells him that [even if there is a storm in Lincolnshire] the ship carrying Hallam's body is sailing on a sea that is as smooth as glass.

XIX. According to Hallam Tennyson this poem was written at Tintern Abbey on the banks of the River Wye.

1. *The Danube*: Hallam died in Vienna; *the Severn*: Hallam was buried at Clevedon, on the River Severn.

7. *And hushes half the babbling Wye*: the tidal water passes from the sea into the Severn, past Clevedon, and on into the Wye, which is tidal for approximately half its length, 'hushing' or stopping its natural flow.

XXXIV. The central idea of this poem is that man must be immortal, or the beauty of the world, and human life itself, would be meaningless and worthless.

XXXV. 2. *narrow house*: the grave.

11. *Aeonian*: existing for ages or aeons. The point of the stanza is the vastness and apparent purposelessness of natural changes.

14. *forgetful shore*: the shore of death.

19. *as Death*: i.e. simply as extinction. The idea is that it is only the hope of immortality which makes man capable of love.

L. The poem expresses a longing for the sense of communion with his dead friend in the dark moments of life.

LIV. An example of Tennyson's religious doubts in conflict with his need to believe.

12. *but*: merely.

20. 'Not able even to say what it is he cries for' (Bradley).

LV. Stanzas 1 and 2: the desire for immortality seems to spring from some divine instinct within us (l. 4), but the evidence of Nature, so careless of the individual life, is strongly to the contrary.

18. *And gather dust and chaff*: i.e. 'in trying to reason' (Bradley).

20. 'My father means by "the larger hope" that the whole human race would through, perhaps, ages of suffering, be at length purified and saved' (Hallam Tennyson).

LVI. The argument is continued from the previous poem. The evidence of fossils found in escarpments and quarries (l. 2.) suggests that Nature cares no more for different kinds or species of life than she does for individual lives. Is man, Nature's highest creation, also doomed to extinction?

6–8. Nature has no concern with man's spirit, only with the facts of life and death.

12. *fanes*: temples.

20. *seal'd within the iron hills*: i.e. 'like any other fossil' (Bradley).

LXVII. 3. *broad water of the west*: the River Severn and its outlet the Bristol Channel. See notes to section XIX.

5. A shaft of moonlight is imagined as coming through a narrow window.

LXXXVI. A spring poem, written at Barmouth, Merioneth, Wales.

6. *dewy-tassel'd*: hung with drops of rain [after the showers].

7. *horned flood*: i.e. 'Between two promontories' (Tennyson). The river is winding and its bank is indented. Cf. 'The Dying Swan', l. 39.

15. *orient star*: 'Any rising star is here intended' (Tennyson).

XCV. The setting is a summer evening in the garden at Somersby. After everyone else has gone to bed Tennyson reads again some of Hallam's letters and, in a 'trance', seems to make contact with Hallam himself.

10. *lit*: alighted.

10–12. *the filmy shapes*, &c.: 'Moths; perhaps the ermine or the puss-moth' (Tennyson).

39. *that which is*: 'the ultimate reality, as distinguished from that half-deceptive appearance which we commonly call the real world' (Bradley). Hallam Tennyson recalls his father saying with deep

emotion, 'Yes, it is true that there are moments when the flesh is nothing to me, when I feel and know the flesh to be the vision, God and the Spiritual the only real and true. Depend upon it, the Spiritual *is* the real: it belongs to one more than the hand and the foot. You may tell me that my hand and my foot are only imaginary symbols of my existence, I could believe you; but you never, never can convince me that the *I* is not an eternal Reality, and that the Spiritual is not the only true and real part of me.' (*Memoir*, ii. 90.)

41. *Aeonian*: see note to section XXXV, l. 11.

46. *matter-moulded*: our normal language, shaped by the need to make statements about this material world, is quite inadequate to describe an experience such as the trance.

CI. Tennyson recalls his childhood memories of Somersby.

4. *burn itself away*: refers to the brilliant reds and browns of the dying leaves in autumn.

11. *lesser wain*: the constellation *ursa minor* which includes the pole-star.

CVI. 32. *the Christ that is to be*: 'The broader Christianity of the future' (Tennyson).

CXV. 2. *quick*: hedge.

3. *squares*: fields.

14. *greening gleam*: i.e. the sea.

CXVI. 4. *the crescent prime*: 'growing Spring' (Tennyson).

6. *re-orient*: risen again.

CXXIII. The vast geological changes which the world undergoes no longer disturb his faith in personal immortality. Cf. section LVI.

CXXIV. 2. 'Present alike in our dearest faith and our ghastliest doubt' (Bradley).

18. *blind clamour*: refers back to lines 10–12.

21–22. *beheld . . . what is*: cf. section XCV, l. 39, and note.

CXXX. Cf. Shelley's *Adonais*, stanza XLII: 'He is made one with Nature.'

PAGE 156. ODE ON THE DEATH OF THE DUKE OF WELLINGTON. See Introduction, pp. 40–41. Sir Charles Tennyson suggests that in order to appreciate this poem fully, 'it should be read (or chanted) aloud with strong emphasis on the rhythm'.

9. *London's central roar*: Wellington was buried in St. Paul's Cathedral, in the City of London.

56. *its blazon'd deeds*: 'Wellington's victories were inscribed in gold letters on the car' (Tennyson).

61. *the dome of the golden cross*: St. Paul's (see note to l. 9).

80–82. These three lines are supposed to be spoken by Lord Nelson, the victor of Trafalgar, who already lay in St. Paul's. He is the 'Mighty Seaman' of l. 84.

99. *the myriads of Assaye*: a reference to Wellington's early campaigns in India. Tennyson notes: 'His first victory was in Hindostan, near this small town, where he defeated the Mahratta army with a force a tenth of their number (1803).'

123. *that loud sabbath*: the battle of Waterloo was fought on Sunday, 18 June 1815.

137. *the Baltic and the Nile*: two of Nelson's victories. The battle of the Baltic (or Copenhagen) was fought in 1801, the battle of the Nile in 1798.

188. *England's Alfred*: King Alfred the Great.

195–7. 'These are full-vowelled lines to describe Fortune emptying her Cornucopia' (Tennyson).

PAGE 166. THE CHARGE OF THE LIGHT BRIGADE. This was an incident during the Crimean War, in which Britain and France were allied against Russia. On 25 October 1854 Lord Cardigan, misunderstanding an order, led the Light Brigade of 607 men in a charge of one and a half miles against a line of Russian artillery, with more Russian artillery ranged on either side. The story of this gallant but futile episode is excellently told in Cecil Woodham-Smith's *The Reason Why* (London, 1953). Tennyson 'founded' the poem on the phrase 'Some one had blundered', which appeared in the original report of the charge in the London *Times*.

PAGE 168. MAUD. 'This poem of "Maud or the Madness" is a little *Hamlet*, the history of a morbid, poetic soul, under the blighting influence of a recklessly speculative age. He is the heir of madness, an egoist with the makings of a cynic, raised to a pure and holy love which elevates his whole nature, passing from the height of triumph to the lowest depth of misery, driven into madness by the loss of her whom he has loved, and, when he has at length passed through the fiery furnace, and has recovered his reason, giving himself up to work for the good of mankind through the unselfishness born of a great passion' (Tennyson).

Part II. II. 'In Brittany. The shell undestroyed amid the storm perhaps symbolises to him his own first and highest nature preserved amid the storms of passion' (Tennyson).

Part II. iv. Tennyson annotated this, 'Haunted (after Maud's death)', and added: ' "O that 'twere possible" appeared first in the *Tribute*, 1837. Sir John Simeon years after begged me to weave a story round this poem, and so *Maud* came into being.'

PAGE 175. THE PASSING OF ARTHUR. This, the final book of *The Idylls of the King*, displays, according to Hallam Tennyson, 'The temporary triumph of evil, the confusion of moral order, closing in the Great Battle of the West.' Of the *Idylls* as a whole Tennyson said: 'My meaning . . . was spiritual. I took the legendary stories of the Round Table as illustrations. I intended Arthur to represent the Ideal Soul of Man coming into contact with the warring elements of the flesh.'

1–2. Sir Bedivere was the first knight created by Arthur at his coronation.

31. *Lancelot's war*: the war between King Arthur and Sir Lancelot; see 'Guinevere', the previous book of the *Idylls*.

35. *an isle of rest*: see l. 427 and note.

51–52. Tennyson annotated these lines: 'The legends which cluster round the King's name.' In 'Guinevere' the 'little elves of chasm and cleft' are described as welcoming the foundation of the Round Table.

56. *Light was Gawain in life*: 'Light' here has the sense of 'immoral'. Tennyson has a low opinion of Gawain: see, for example, the part Gawain plays in the idyll 'Pelleas and Ettarre'.

59. *Modred*: the nephew of Arthur and the leader of the revolt against his rule.

77. *One lying the dust at Almesbury*: Guinevere, Arthur's queen, retired to a convent at Almesbury after the discovery of her adulterous relationship with Sir Lancelot. In 'Guinevere' there is a description of Arthur's visit to the convent, when Guinevere fell on the ground before him and 'grovell'd with her face against the floor'.

81. *sunset bound*: western limit, where the sun sets; *Lyonnesse*: the mythical land said to have been submerged by the sea off Cornwall.

87. *circle*: horizon.

90–91. i.e. the winter solstice.

148. *and so the dead have kings*: assuming there are kings among the dead.

170. The section based on the earlier 'Morte d'Arthur' begins at this point; it ends on l. 440.

184. *Such a sleep*: i.e. the sleep of death.

189. *Camelot*: the seat of King Arthur's court.

191. *Merlin*: the great magician and seer of Arthurian legend.

195. *Excalibur*: the name of King Arthur's sword, given to him by the Lady of the Lake (see ll. 271-4).

199. *samite*: a rich dress-material of silk.

243. *fĕalty*: fidelity, the duty owed to a feudal superior.

248. *lief*: beloved.

254. *chased*: worked.

278. *clouded with his own conceit*: deceived by his own false thinking.

307. *streamer of the northern morn*: the Aurora Borealis or Northern Lights.

308. *the moving isles of winter*: icebergs.

316. *drawing thicker breath*: 'breathing more heavily' (Tennyson).

366. *Three Queens*: in Malory they are identified as Morgan le Fay (Arthur's sister), the Queen of Northgalis, and the Queen of the Waste Lands.

381-2. An allusion to the fading of the moonlight at sunrise.

383. *greaves and cuisses*: leg-armour and thigh-armour.

383-4. *drops Of onset*: drops of blood shed in the battle.

419 *That nourish a blind life within the brain*: that live a life of unreason.

427. *Avilion*: Avalon; in Celtic legend, an island in the western seas which was an earthly paradise and the resting place of heroes.

434-7. A reference to the legend that swans sing only once, when they are about to die (cf. 'The Dying Swan').

445. In 'The Coming of Arthur', the first book of *The Idylls of the King*, these words are spoken by Merlin the magician at the time of Arthur's birth. Cf. Tennyson's observation on the *Idylls* as a whole: '[It] is the dream of man coming into practical life and ruined by one sin. Birth is a mystery and death is a mystery, and in the midst lies the tableland of life, and its struggles and performances. It is not the history of one man or of one generation but of a whole cycle of generations.'

454. *that high day*: the day of the founding of the Round Table described in 'The Coming of Arthur'.

457-61. The 'dawn', says Tennyson, represents 'the East, whence have sprung all the great religions of the world. A triumph of welcome is given to him who has proved himself "more than conqueror".'

468. *From less to less and vanish into light*: 'The purpose of the individual man may fail for a time, but his work cannot die' (Tennyson).

PAGE 191. 'FLOWER IN THE CRANNIED WALL'. 'The flower was plucked out of a wall at "Waggoners Wells," near Haslemere' (Tennyson).

PAGE 191. 'IN THE GARDEN AT SWAINSTON'. Swainston is near Newport, in the Isle of Wight; it was the home of Tennyson's great friend Sir John Simeon, who died abroad in 1870 (cf. l. 7: 'The Master was far away'). Tennyson was profoundly distressed by Simeon's death: see Sir Charles Tennyson: *Alfred Tennyson*, pp. 388–9. The two other dead friends celebrated in the poem are Henry Lushington and Arthur Hallam.

PAGE 192. TO VIRGIL. Virgil died at Brundisium in 19 B.C. on his return from a visit to some of the scenes in the eastern Mediterranean which he had presented in his verse.

6. *he that sang the Works and Days*: Hesiod, an early Greek poet, wrote an agricultural poem, *Works and Days*, which was imitated by Virgil in his *Georgics*.

13. *Tityrus*: a shepherd in Virgil's *Eclogues*; the allusion is to the opening line of *Ecologue* i.

15–16. The 'poet-satyr' is Silenus. In Virgil's *Eclogue* vi two shepherds tie up Silenus with his own garlands while he is in a drunken sleep and only release him when he has sung for them. Most of the *Eclogue* is taken up with his song.

17. *Pollio*: Gaius Asinus Pollio, Roman Consul in 40 B.C. Virgil dedicated to him his 'Messianic Eclogue' (*Eclogue* iv), which forecasts the coming of a Golden Age and has sometimes been regarded as a prophecy of the Birth of Christ.

27. *Golden branch*: a reference to the sixth book of Virgil's *Aeneid* and to the magical Golden Bough which Aeneas plucks before descending to the underworld.

36. An allusion to *Eclogue* i. 66, which reflects the ancient belief, now substantiated, that Britain was once joined to the continent of Europe.

37. *Mantovano*: Mantuan.

PAGE 194. 'FRATER AVE ATQUE VALE'. 'Written in 1880 when my father and I visited Sirmione, the peninsula of Catullus on the Lago di Garda' (Hallam Tennyson). Gaius Valerius Catullus (*c.* 84–*c.* 54 B.C.) was one of Tennyson's favourite Latin poets; two of his most famous poems are 'Ave atque vale', written for his dead brother, and the lines to

Sirmio, an expression of joy on homecoming. Tennyson's own brother, Charles, had died in 1879.

PAGE 194. RIZPAH. For the title of this poem see 2 Samuel xxi. 10. Tennyson notes that the poem was based on a paragraph in a penny magazine, *Old Brighton*, which had been lent to him by a friend. Hallam Tennyson supplies us with the original paragraph, which is about the mother of a young man who had been hanged in chains for a highway robbery and his corpse left on the gallows: 'When the elements had caused the clothes and flesh to decay, his aged mother, night after night, in all weathers, and the more tempestuous the weather the more frequent the visits, made a sacred pilgrimage to the lonely spot on the Downs, and it was noticed that on her return she always brought something away with her in her apron. Upon being watched it was discovered that the bones of the hanging man were the objects of her search, and as the wind and rain scattered them on the ground she conveyed them to her home. There she kept them, and, when the gibbet was stripped of its horrid burden, in the dead silence of the night she interred them in the hallowed enclosure of Old Shoreham Churchyard. What a sad story of a Brighton Rizpah!'

PAGE 200. VASTNESS.

36. *him*: 'The last line means "What matters anything in this world without faith in the immortality of the soul and of Love?" ' (Tennyson). In this line 'him' is usually taken to refer to Arthur Hallam, but Tennyson may have been thinking of his brother Charles.

PAGE 203. CROSSING THE BAR. 'Made in my father's eighty-first year, after his serious illness in 1888–9, on a day in October 1889, while crossing the Solent, as we came from Aldworth to Farringford. When he repeated it to me in the evening, I said, "That is the crown of your life's work." He answered, "It came in a moment." ' (Hallam Tennyson).

15. *I hope to see my Pilot face to face*: 'The pilot has been on board all the while, but in the dark I have not seen him' (Tennyson). Hallam Tennyson adds, 'He explained the Pilot as "that Divine and Unseen Who is always guiding us". A few days before his death he said to me, "Mind you put my *Crossing the Bar* at the end of all editions of my poems." '